Ales Hrdlicka

Anthropological Investigations on one Thousand White and Colored Children of Both Sexes

the inmates of the New York Juvenile Asylum, with additional notes on

one hundred colored children of the New York colored orphan asylum

Ales Hrdlicka

Anthropological Investigations on one Thousand White and Colored Children of Both Sexes
the inmates of the New York Juvenile Asylum, with additional notes on one hundred colored children of the New York colored orphan asylum

ISBN/EAN: 9783337367657

Printed in Europe, USA, Canada, Australia, Japan

Cover: Foto ©Andreas Hilbeck / pixelio.de

More available books at **www.hansebooks.com**

ANTHROPOLOGICAL INVESTIGATIONS

ON

One Thousand White and Colored Children of Both Sexes

The Inmates of the New York Juvenile Asylum,

With Additional Notes on One Hundred Colored Children of the New York Colorec Orphan Asylum.

By Dr. ALES HRDLICKA.

The following work is based upon the investigations of one thousand children of the New York Juvenile Asylum and on about one hundred additional cases of children of the New York Colored Orphan Asylum.

Before proceeding to state the results of my investigations, I think it advisable to make a few remarks about the real nature, principal objects, and mode of execution of the work.

There were measured and examined, as thoroughly as possible without offense to the modesty of the children, one thousand of the inmates of the institution. In addition, as already mentioned, a number of the most important measurements were secured on about one hundred negro children, inmates of the New York Colored Orphan Asylum.

In selecting the measurements to be applied to the children I have chosen all those which can be expected to show the principal characteristics of the children's evolution, and I have excluded all those which are either of a secondary importance, or very difficult, or uncertain of execution. The following measures were taken on each child:

1. Height.
2. Sitting height.
3. Arm expanse.
4. Weight.
5. Depth of the chest (at the height of the nipples).
6. Width of the chest (at the same height).
7. Maximum circumference of the head.
8. The greatest length of the head.
9. The greatest width of the head.
10. The height of the head (from meati line).

11. Diameter bi-auricular of the head (the width of the head in front and a little above the tragus of the ears).

12. The smallest width of the forehead.

In addition to these measurements, the average pressure and traction force of each child in each of its hands was secured.

The child having been measured, was subjected to a thorough inspection. The inspection in boys comprised every part of the body. This was also the case in the very small girls. In girls above eight, the private parts of the body remained carefully covered.

In addition to the body, the structures in the mouth were examined, and finally the lungs and the heart were submitted to careful percussion and auscultation.

To all examination-records were appended the most essential facts from the history of the child and its family.

The Object of the Investigations.

The principal aim of these investigations, briefly expressed, is to learn as much as possible about the physical state of the children who are being admitted and kept in juvenile asylums.

In the second place, this study is a part of the general anthropological work of the author and thus expected to result in an addition to our knowledge of the normal child, and of several classes of children who are, morally or otherwise, abnormal.

It is well known that many of the children admitted into the juvenile asylums come from very poor classes of people. The second large contingent of the inmates are children who have been sent to the institution as incorrigible or even criminal. Both these classes of children are from sociological point of view abnormal, and it is important to learn how far their physical characteristics correspond to their moral character.

It is self-evident that if either or both of the two classes of children were found to correspond physically to their social or moral state, that is, if they were physically inferior to other children of the same sex and similar age, then these subjects would have to be considered as generally handicapped in the struggle of life. The only thing which could be done for such children in an institution like the Juvenile Asylum would be to more or less compensate for their natural defects. Under such circumstances the asylum would be no more than a correctional institute and could never turn out normal children who would be fully capable of wrestling with the difficulties with which they will be confronted in life. If such is the case, the community could not expect to greatly improve them in the short term of two or three years, but would have to take very much prolonged additional care of these individuals.

If, on the other hand, the inmates of the Juvenile Asylum are not found to differ greatly in their strength and constitution from the average ordinary children, and thus not be handicapped by serious physical defects—then the state of these children will be very much more hopeful. The community could in this case expect that a course of proper training and instruction, such a course as it tries to provide for these children in the Juvenile Asylum, would be largely sufficient to elevate or reform these children and to allow them to reach the normal average standard of boys and girls of their ages. Individuals of this kind would be on an almost equal footing in facing the problems of their lives with other individuals who have never been socially or morally inferior, and they would be almost as fully capable as these other children to become good and useful members of the community. In this case it is plain that no expense which the community might undergo to elevate and improve the inmates of the Juvenile Asylum would be lost; furthermore, the community would be sure that every additional expense for the benefit of this class of individuals would not be misapplied, but could be expected to bring its proper returns.

It is true that actual experience may have already largely illustrated the problems just stated by showing what percentage of the discharged inmates of the Juvenile Asylum have become self supporting men and women and good members of society; but science, which will give us an intimate knowledge of every individual child admitted, will effect more than mere experience alone could ever do. A thorough knowledge of the subjects concerned, of the children who are being committed to and discharged from our juvenile asylums, will alone sufficiently clear up the problem of what future can be expected for these children. Such a knowledge ought to guide us very largely in establishing the most efficient means to secure for these children the best future that it may be possible to provide for them.

Besides benefiting the whole class of children concerned, such investigations as have been undertaken on the inmates of the New York Juvenile Asylum will also benefit the examined subjects individually and immediately.

If we should examine any given class of children in a thorough way, we would find, now and then, in some individuals of the class, certain small, physical deficiencies or irregularities, either natural or acquired. We should find frequently, for instance, no matter how normal mentally the class of children examined might be, and to what social class it might belong, such abnormalities as adherence of the prepuce in the boys, or as drooping shoulders on one side of the body, due to habitual faulty positions, or a faulty position of some of the teeth, etc. Most of the irregularities of these kinds can, under the appropriate direction, be corrected, and such a correction undoubtedly benefits the individual. It will be seen from the following report how useful in these directions our examinations have been.

So far I have spoken only of the direct advantages of the investigations, but there are further and by no means secondary advantages resulting from the same which are purely of a scientific nature. This point will be best appreciated by a perusal of the report itself. It will be seen that we have gained certain interesting data concerning the evolution of the children in different ages. This study enables us to state for the first time the physical differences in all parts of the body between the white and colored children. The records will also give us some notion as to the structural differences among the children of several nationalities, etc. The majority of the following data, however, should not be looked upon as definite conclusions on the particular subject which they may concern. They are really but indications of what can be expected from prolonged studies in the same direction.

The Mode of Execution of the Work.

In conducting examinations of this extent, the first and very important condition is to properly arrange the recording of the data.

Measurements.

N. Y. JUVENILE ASYLUM, Anthropological Examinations and Measurements.   Accession No. of Sheet .... Sex .... Ages .... Date ....

NAME	No.	SEX.	AGE	Height.	Sitting Height.	Arm Expanse	Weight.	Femur on R. Hand	Femur on L. Hand	Tension Force	CHEST.		HEAD.						CONDITIONS HEAD	FACE.	EARS	NOSE	TEETH	PALATE	UVULA	Spine	LIMBS	BODY	GENITALS	LOWER	REMARK	REMARKS
											D. & F. at 18 Mo.	O. Lat. at 18 Mo.	Length Circum. Meas.	D. & P. Hor.	In. Lat. Diam.	D. Br. Vert.	B. Arrow Hor.	Region of the Head														

My system of doing this was the following: I would have a reliable clerk sitting behind a screen in the same room where I conduct the examinations, and to this clerk I would dictate in a systematic way the condition of part after part of the body of the subject examined. To this record would later be joined the measures of the subject. After the examination and measuring have been recorded on the sheet, the same was completed with such case-book data concerning the subject as were considered to be of importance and reliable.

All the records concerning an individual would be kept on one separate sheet. These individual sheets make it very easy to arrange the subjects, before tabulating the data, according to any prime condition required (such as sex, age, etc.).

The next important step in working on the records is their proper tabulation. In order to facilitate this I constructed sheets of which I give here an illustration. The advantages of such sheets are too evident to be dilated upon. Such an arrangement enables us to handle whole groups of subjects with almost as much ease and with equal precision as we would handle an individual.

It is hardly necessary for me to state that I made personally all the examinations. This is the best way in which to assure a perfect uniformity of the work and a full value of the results therefrom.

As to the measurements, I have received valuable aid from Mr. W. R. Buchanan, one of the attendants of the institution.

All measuring was done with modern and well tested instruments. Mr. Buchanan received thorough instruction in the matter from me, and his measures were not allowed to stand as valid until I had satisfied myself that his errors in successive measurements on the same person were reduced to a minimum, and that he had a thorough understanding of what he was doing. Even then, in order to insure a full reliability of the measurements, in all cases where a certain measurement was found to differ from time to time through conditions on the part of the individual measured (such as for instance was the case with the height, the chest, and the force measurements), I have allowed to be stated only the average of three measures secured at different periods. In addition, I satisfied myself from time to time by re-measuring some of the children that the data obtained by Mr. Buchanan remain correct. Such precautions, with an intelligent, patient and interested man, and good instruments, could not but secure precision.

The children without a single exception on the part of the boys and with a very few exceptions on the part of the girls were happy to submit to the examinations. The few cases of girls in which any objections existed were promptly excused from the necessity of being examined.

In no single case was there observed even a temporary bad effect of any kind on the minds of the children as a result of the examinations. I beg to accentuate this fact, as very frequently the possibility of such an effect has a deterring influence on the authorities of schools or institutions where there are no other objections to investigations on the inmates.

Arrangement of the Records.

The study will be presented in several sections, which are calculated to throw some light on distinct groups of children.

Part I. General data on the total of subjects.—The children in this group are separated only according to sex and color.

Part II. Detailed study.—Children in this group are separated according to their color, sexes and ages.

Part III. Physical differences between white and colored children of both sexes and different ages.

Part IV. Children of different nationalities.—Subjects divided according to their sexes and ages.

Part V. Children without any physical defects, with their family and individual histories.

Part VI. Children with five or more physical abnormalities.

Part VII. Vicious and criminal children.

Part VIII. Children whose parents were intemperate, prostitute or criminal.

Part IX. Children both of whose parents are dead.

Part. X. Children one or both of whose parents died of consumption.

PART I.

General Observations on the Total of Characters of the White and of the Colored Children.

There were no systematic observations made on the inmates of the Juvenile Asylum, but I took every occasion to come into a close contact with the children and to learn as much as possible about their moral status, their habits and their health. The observations thus collected were confirmed by inquiries among the teachers and attendants of the children; and I have received especially valuable assistance in this respect from the Superintendent of the Institution, Dr. Bruce. In a general way I can sum up the observations as follows:

When the children are admitted into the institution, they are almost invariably in some way, both morally and physically, inferior to healthy children from good social classes at large. A closer observation, however, reveals the fact that the inferiorities of the children who are becoming inmates of the Juvenile Asylum, are in the majority of cases only the results of neglect, or of improper nutrition, or of both these causes combined. Many of the children are more or less neglected, or spoiled, or less developed or strong, than they should be; but a really inferior child, that is, an inherently vicious, or an imbecile child, or a child who could not be much improved by better food and better hygienic surroundings, is a very rare exception.

Within a month, at most, after the admission of the child into the Asylum, and sometimes within a week, decided changes for the better are observed in almost every instance. Among the first improvements noticed in the children are better appetite and better appearance; while from the moral standpoint it is noticeable that the children stop using foul language, show more obedience, and manifest much less disposition to lying and pilfering.

What is a very important fact, and at the same time the best evidence of the real character of these children, is that after their admission, gradually, all of the individuals of the same sex and age become more and more alike, and show less and less of their former diversity. Each child, of course, preserves the fundamental differences of its nature, but it loses gradually more and more of those conditions, both physical and moral, which distinguished it acutely from the healthy and well-trained children, as well as from the individuals confined a longer time in the institution. These changes, although taking place on the basis of rule and advice, are not due to compulsion. One of the most important factors in this improvement of the newly admitted subjects, I have noticed to be spontaneous emulation by the newcomers of the already improved habits of the children who have been here longer. After the first few weeks of residence the children settle well down to the life of the institution, and they can seldom be seen in any but a happy state of mind and good disposition.

In learning, the newcomers are generally found to be more or less retarded when brought to school in the institution, but in a great majority of cases they begin to acquire rapidly, and a child usually reaches the average standard of the class to which it is allotted. An inveterate backwardness in learning is not noticeable, except in a few instances.

The advance of the children continues slowly in all directions during their stay in the asylum. When the time of discharge comes, the children have certainly all more or less improved. I have had occasion to satisfy myself of this fact by re-examining a number of the subjects immediately before they were discharged, and although the periods since the first examination of the same individuals amounted to only from three to six months, nevertheless in every case a general improvement, both physically and in the behavior of the child, was noticeable.

I cannot say, however, that every child is discharged from the New York Juvenile Asylum only when all the improvement of which he or she was in need, or which was possible with them, has been achieved. Undoubtedly many of the children are discharged *before* the full good, both physical and moral, has been effected.

It is widely different to teach a habit to a child, and to inculcate this habit so that it becomes a firm part of its nature. The child, who has been many times well compared with a young tree, which you can bend in any direction, can be corrected of bad habits and taught good ones, and can in addition be physically much improved in a comparatively short time. But the child will lose these advantages as rapidly as it has acquired them if it comes into circumstances which favor their loss. Only such a child will be safe against losing the benefits given to it by the institution, in whom the body has been permanently strengthened and in whom the good habits have been so firmly inculcated that they become a stable component part of its nature.

To improve a child to the degree just expressed requires a much longer time than is necessary simply to teach the child better habits and elevate its physical condition. The length of time necessary to effect the complete restoration of the child (and this, I think, is the only true duty and the only true charity of society), will vary largely with different individuals, and can only be determined by a constant and careful observation of each subject by his attendants, his teacher and his physician.

I will not enter here into further details.

That what I said above is true, is well demonstrated by the frequent recurrences in cases where the discharged child returned to similar circumstances in which it lived before coming into the Juvenile Asylum. Fortunately in a very large number of instances the child gets a new home in which the good circumstances initiated in the asylum continue until the child is out of danger of recurrence.

Examinations.

Of the 1,000 children examined, 700 were boys and 300 were girls. Of the boys 634 were white and 66 colored. The girls include 274 white and 26 colored children.

In age the white boys ranged from 5 to 17 years, the white girls from 5 to 18. The colored boys from 6 to 16, and the colored girls from 7 to 15 years.

The methods of examination have already been explained. All such parts examined which were found to agree well with the typical form of the same parts in healthy children of corresponding color, sex and age, were recorded as normal. As an *abnormality* everything was characterized which was a decided deviation from the typical form in health of the particular part examined.

The recorded abnormalities comprised two principal classes of characters: First, Those characters whose origin can be referred to some irregularity or defect in the principles from which the child originates, (that is in the paternal sperm or in the maternal ovule,) or to the embryonic evolution of the individual. And second, All those characters whose origin is subsequent to the origin period of the being, and which develop mostly after the birth of the child.

The first class of abnormalities is generally termed inherited, or congenital, or inborn, while characters of the second class are called acquired abnormalities.

The abnormalities of the second class here defined are principally the results of early pathological processes, or they may be due to the habits of the individual. The pathological conditions which most frequently are the source of such subsequent abnormalities in a child are above all the various degrees of rachitis, and then early paralyses.

Abnormalities due to habit are usually developed by the individual using one arm or one foot or some other part of the body much in excess to the other limb or other parts, or by habitual improper holding of the body.

In the case of younger children, the subject will frequently allow one of his shoulders to droop more than the other. Or the child will support itself more on one lower limb than on the other, and as a consequence acquire a lateral inclination of the pelvis, or of the spine. Other children will habitually hold their heads too low or to one side and acquire stooping shoulders, or a faulty position of the head.

In other children the nature of the work which they begin to do frequently gives rise to habitual faulty positions of some part of the body, which may ultimately result in established deformities. As an example of abnormalities of this kind I may again mention drooping shoulders, pelvic inclinations, and even depressions of certain parts of the chest, such as occur particularly in shoemakers.

The *significance* and *gravity* of the various abnormalities differ considerably. This problem can be viewed either objectively or subjectively.

The objective significance of atypical characters, that is, the mean-

ing of the abnormalities of a being when we consider the standing of
that being in a class of similar individuals, is quite uncertain and is
being still generally much discussed. *As a matter of fact there are
very few abnormalities which we can observe in man that may be
positively said to render the individual generally either decidedly inferior or markedly superior to his fellow beings. No single physical abnormality (and but a rare combination of abnormalities) suffices
of itself to stamp any individual as a human degenerate.*

It may be said that the great majority of the inborn abnormalities
still elude our comprehension, and from what experience teaches us
we must assume that these characters, as well as numbers of acquired abnormalities, are largely without any objective significance.

As examples of inborn characters without any known or traceable
significance may be mentioned the abnormalities we observe on the
toes and those of the external ear.

A certain objective effect may in some cases be due to the dis-
figurement to which some abnormalities give rise.

The subjective effects of abnormalities differ very largely. They
differ according to the situation of the abnormalities and according
to their extent. The malformation of some part of the body may
not only have a depressing effect on the individual who possesses it,
but it may also interfere with his work or other functions. Ob-
liquely set eyes, for instance, or even a case of pronounced strabismus, may, at least for a time, cause considerable worry, depression
and inconvenience to their owner; while a deformed limb may interfere with the walking, or, in the case of the hand, the deformity
may prove to be a serious hindrance to the acquisition of certain
handicrafts by the individual and thus be a serious personal dis-
advantage. If the abnormality concerns the head, it may prove of
even graver subjective consequences to the being than if any of the
limbs are affected. If, for example, as a result of rachitis or some
other pathological process, there occurs a very premature union of
the cranial sutures, the sequellae of this may favor a decadence of
the mental powers of the individual, and possibly even render him
imbecile. Curvatures of the spine or of other bones may cause the
individual many a difficulty in his life, and certain abnormalities of
the genital organs may result in unpleasant and even serious conse-

quences. On the other hand, a large number of abnormalities, and especially those of congenital nature, have very little or no traceable subjective effect on their bearer.

What has just been said is principally for the purpose of affording indications as to how to properly view the abnormalities we may meet in the inmates of the New York Juvenile Asylum.

It should be kept in mind, first of all, that many of the abnormalities of which we shall speak are simply the results of states of malnutrition, or of certain pathological conditions, and do not indicate inferiority any more than would a pale skin after a hemorrhage or so many scars after wounds.

In the second place, a great many of those abnormalities in our children, which are really due to some defects or peculiarities of either of the parental principles from which the being springs, are, so far as we know, without any practical significance, either objective or subjective.

Third, it is a fact, although we have no real statistics on this point, that any of the abnormalities met with in this institution can also be met with occasionally in the children of any class or social position.

And fourth, the real object of the exposure of the abnormalities of these children is not only to show their physical standing, but also to show the way to repair or compensate for the inborn defects, or the consequences of previous afflictions of these individuals.

We will now approach the data obtained by the examinations. In this place only the total figures will be given; the details will be found in the various sections of the study.

Among the 634 white males examined, 58, or a little over 9 per cent., show no abnormality whatever on any part of their body. Among the 274 white girls examined, there were 35, or almost 13 per cent., on whose body there was nothing atypical. From among the 66 negro boys, 5, or 7.6 per cent., were entirely normal, while out of the 26 colored girls there were 7, or almost 27 per cent., who showed no irregularities.

Thus about one-seventh of all the inmates of the New York Juvenile Asylum are without a blemish on their bodies. This proportion may perhaps seem somewhat small to those who are not accustomed to close examinations of either children or adults. Those who have closely examined numerous individuals know that a body perfect in all its parts is rare in any class of either young subjects or grown people. This fact can be appreciated by every intelligent observer, even though he be not an anthropologist, if he will closely scrutinize his acquaintances, or his friends, and even himself and his own children. He will see so many irregular ears, teeth, heads, faces, etc., that instead of regarding 14 per cent. as too small a percentage of normality, he will wonder at the extent of this proportion.

It will be noticed from the above figures that the girls show a better physical standing in both the white and colored children, and also that the colored boys seem to be physically somewhat inferior to the white ones. But it should be remembered in the first place that we have not examined the genital organs and the gluteal region of the female children. If we eliminate these same items with the boys, we obtain as entirely typical 89, or 14 per cent., of the white, and 7, or 10.6 per cent., of the colored subjects, which proportions are nearer to those obtained in the girls. I hardly doubt but that, would we examine also the above-mentioned parts in the female children, the proportion of abnormalities in the two sexes would be nearly alike. As to the somewhat greater apparent inferiority of the colored boys, I am afraid that the number of these examined is too small to allow us to form any definite conclusions. It has been always my experience, in examinations outside of the Juvenile Asylum, to find the negroes in the average physically superior to the whites and possessing less of abnormalities, which fact is also well exemplified in our colored girls, and will be shown in the item where will be stated the proportions of abnormalities to the different groups of children with the same abnormalities.

Out of the remaining children, that is, those who show one or several atypical physical characters, there were 112, or 17.7 per cent., white, and 11, or 16.7 per cent., colored boys, and 72, or 26.3 per cent., white, and 5, or 19.2 per cent., colored girls, who presented only one single abnormality. The abnormality which these children showed was in many cases but a slight one, and we really ought to count most of the individuals of this group among the entirely normal subjects.

The number of physically inferior children is not easy to ascertain.

We have two distinct criteria by which to determine an abnormal subject, namely, the gravity of the atypical characters the individual presents, or simply the number of these characters. Neither of these criteria is entirely satisfactory. We have not the knowledge to be able to judge of the exact significance and gravity of every abnormality; and, on the other hand, the simple number of irregularities on a body does not express their import and hence the real state of the body. However, the latter criterion, which deals with the numbers and not the gravity of the abnormalities, is to be here preferred as about equally efficient to the first and very much more simple and certain.

How many atypical characters ought a subject to have in order to be considered an exception among the average children? There is no pre-established standard for this, and the formation of our standard will be quite arbitrary. On the basis of general scientific principles, and as a result of a thorough study of the subject in question, I think it will be safe to mark all those children as exceptional in whom more than one-half of the parts of the body examined presented each one or more abnormalities.   '

There were of such children 62, or 9.8 per cent., among the white, and 8, or 12.1 per cent., among the colored boys, and 16, or 5.8 per cent., among the white, and 1, or 3.8 per cent., among the colored girls.

There is not much difference—at least no difference which we have not already observed—according to the color of the children; but there is a decided difference between the males and the females of both the whites and the negroes, the females showing a much smaller proportion of subjects with numerous abnormalities.

The percentages of children in this class are not very extraordinary. It should be noticed that if we take away the two extremes, the physically entirely normal individuals and those with many abnormalities, that we have remaining fully four-fifths of all the children examined as those with intermediary conditions. Should we, for the sake of illustration, express the physical condition of the children by such terms is fine, medium and bad, the fine and bad would embrace in all 192 individuals, while 808 would remain as medium.

Male Children. White & Colored.

No of Abnormalities:

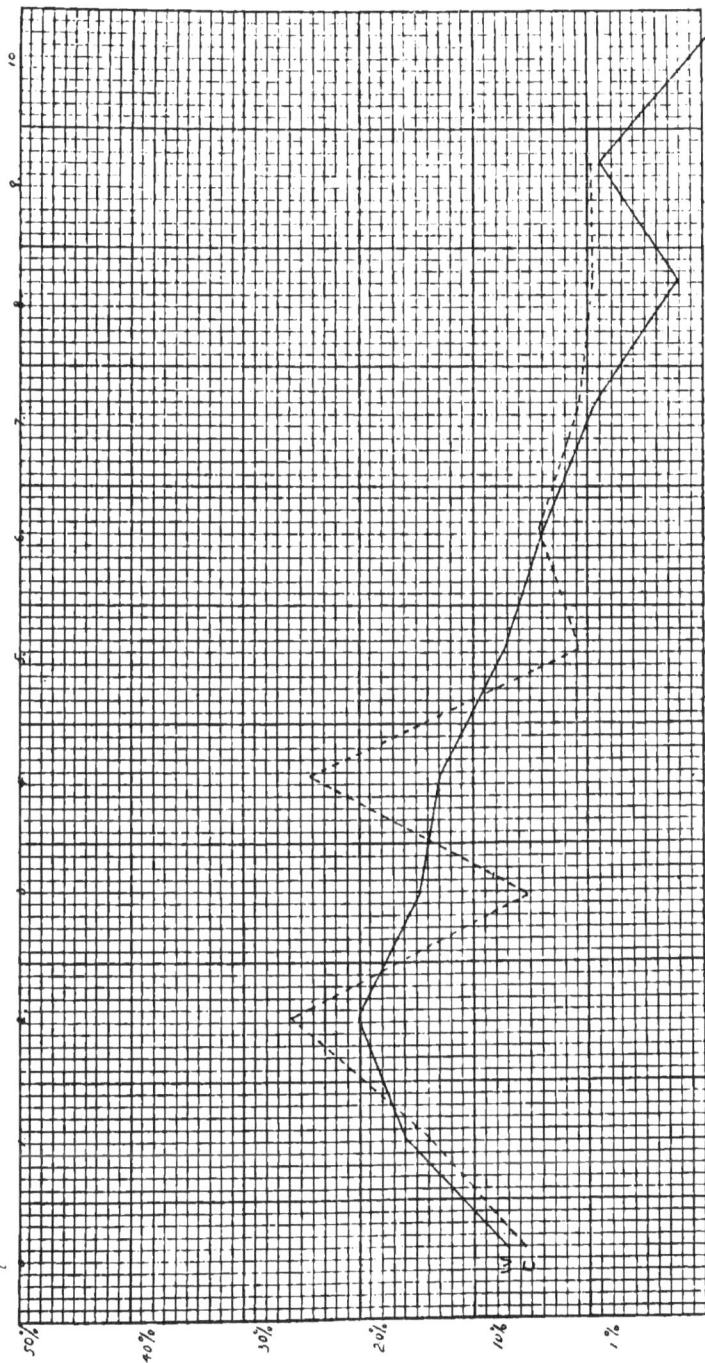

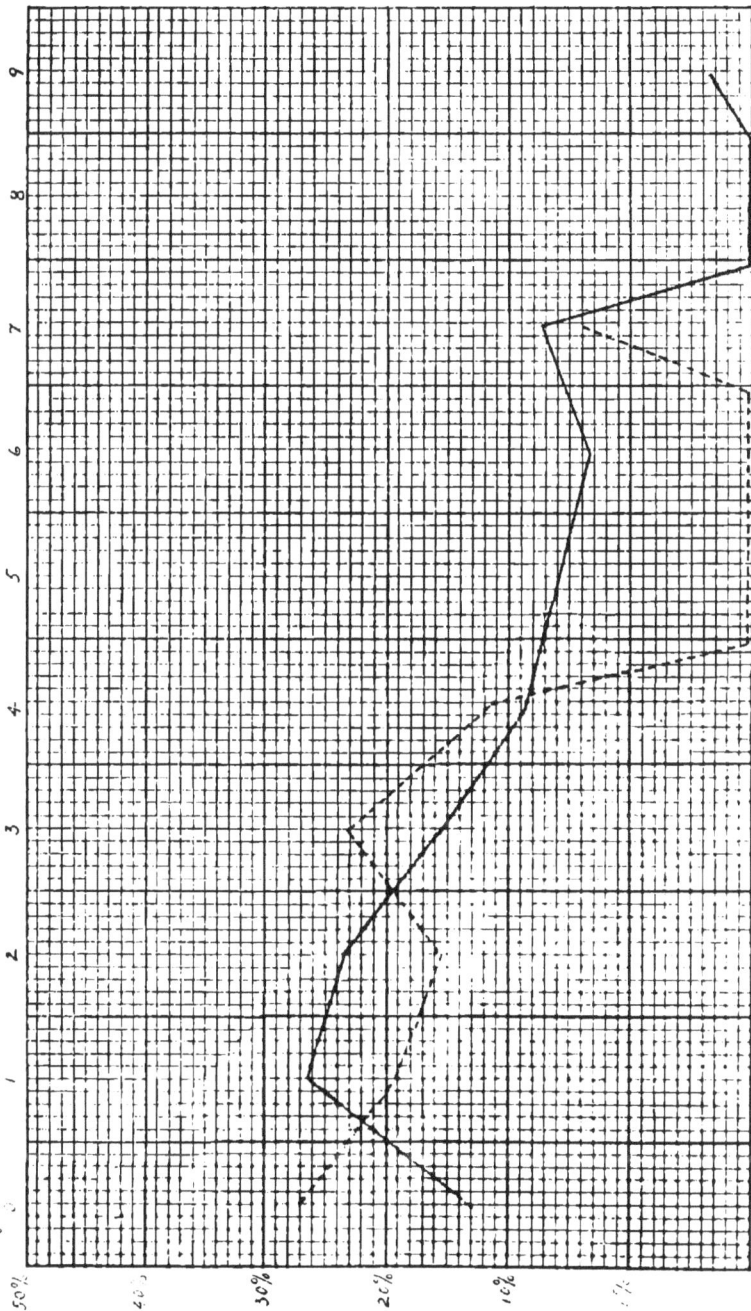

No. of Abnormalities

The average proportion of abnormalities to the whole number of subjects with same were found to be as follows: Proportion to each white boy, 2.71; to each colored boy, 2.60; to each white girl, 2.33; to each colored girl, 2.05.

I doubt very much whether similarly careful and extensive records on any 1,000 ordinary children of similar ages outside of the institution would show figures greatly different from those above. Of course, in the children of the wealthy classes we may find that certain of the abnormalities have been corrected by the physician, dentist, oculist or trainer.

Excluding the children in whom one-half or more of the parts of the body examined show some abnormality, I think it would be safe to consider the remaining inmates of the asylum, so far as abnormalities are concerned, as fairly average children.

The different number of abnormalities observed in different subjects give us a basis for several interesting curves which illustrate very nicely the averages and the extremes of the physical condition of the children, according to their color and sexes. These curves, which do not need much comment, are here reproduced. We can notice principally the aggregation of the bulk of the children within the first three or four columns, that is, near to the normal. It can be seen, further, that all the curves in the white and in the colored, and in the males as well as in the females, present almost the same figure.

The somewhat more erratic curves in the negroes are undoubtedly due to small numbers of individuals which enter into their formation.

The next step in the analysis of the observed abnormalities will be a division of these characters according to the parts of the body on which they were detected.

I will give here several rows of figures which will show the percentage of the abnormalities on each separate part of the body in the white children, and next to these I will place similar percentages obtained on negro children. The latter figures are still somewhat influenced by the small number of subjects.

These data have no relation to the amount of abnormalities observed in the different classes of children. They simply express the relative frequency of the various irregularities in different portions of the body.

2

The table is arranged in such a way that the white males are taken as a standard for the headings, and we proceed from the minimum of percentages to the maximum of same:

Percentage of Abnormalities of the Different Parts of the Body, with Reference to the Total of Abnormalities.

	White male.	White male, genital abnormalities excluded.	White female.	Colored male.	Colored male, genital abnormalities excluded.	Colored female.
	%	%	%	%	%	%
Scalp	.....	.....	0.20	.....	.....	.....
Eyes (strabismus only)	0.90	1 09	1.(7	.....	.....	.....
Hair	1.75	2.09	3.05	0.64	0.76	.....
Forehead	2.47	2.95	1 61	0.64	0.76	.....
Limbs	5.12	6 15	8.24	9.55	11 53	12.20
Head	5.36	6 43	6 45	3.18	3.84	4.90
Teeth	7.47	8 97	8.96	9 55	11.53	4.90
Uvula	7.60	9.11	10.75	8 28	10.00	7.32
Face	7.78	9.33	5.73	9.55	11 53	2.44
Body	8.02	9.62	5 56	12.74	15 38	14.63
Gums	9 76	11.72	12.00	6.37	7 09	9.75
Ears	13.32	15.99	15 77	12 74	15.38	19.50
Palate	13.74	20.83	20.40	9.55	11.53	25.00
Genitals	16.70	.....	.....	17.20	.....	.....

It appears from the above table that more abnormalities are found in both white and colored children on the parts about the head, including the face and the mouth, than on all the rest of the body. Abnormalities of the palate, the ear, and particularly those of the male genitals, are the most frequent.

In but a very few parts of the body is there any decided difference in the percentages of the abnormalities between the two sexes. Atypical forms of the palate are relatively much more frequent in the female than they are in the male, which fact is especially noticeable in the colored children.

The forehead was found more frequently deformed in the male, both white and colored. The limbs are somewhat more often abnormal in some respect in the females, again in both white and colored. The teeth of the colored girls appear to be more regular than those of the colored boys. The face is decidedly more often abnormal in the boys. The bodies of the white girls appear to be in average more free from irregularities than the bodies of the white boys; in the colored children we notice no difference.

FIG. 3.—Advanced scaphocephaly. Due to premature union of sagittal suture, as a consequence of which the head becomes very long and narrow.

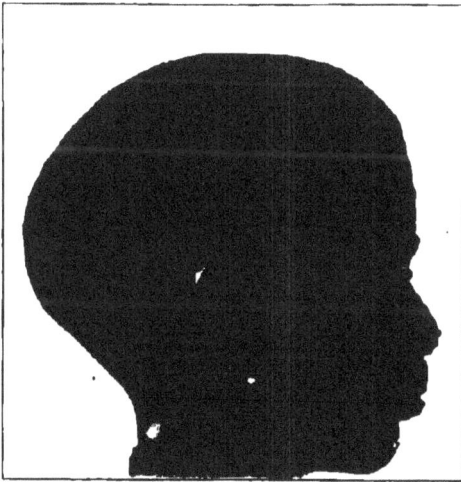

FIG. 3.—Lateral View.

The differences between the white and the colored children are not as well defined as they would be if we had sufficient numbers of the colored subjects. It will be noticed, however, that among the colored children there were found none with strabismus; further, that the head of the colored children in both sexes shows less frequent irregularities, and the limbs, also, in both sexes, more frequent irregularities, than is the case in the white children. The teeth and the face in the colored girls are less frequently affected than they are among the white girls. The differences in the palate, which seem so apparent are chiefly due to the small number of the colored subjects.

I will give next *the varieties of abnormalities which were observed in connection with the different parts of the body.* In this case we will follow the parts of the body in the order in which they were inspected. Abnormalities about the serious nature of which there is no doubt will be printed in italics.

Abnormalities of the Head.

	WHITE.		COLORED.	
	Male.	Female.	Male.	Female.
Number of children examined	634	274	66	26
Total number of abnormalities	89	36	5	2
Head very large (after a hydrocephalus)	1	....	....	....
Head very high	1	1	1	....
Head very narrow	......	1	....	....
Head asymetrical, or irregular	19	4	....	....
Scaphocephalus	3	2	1	....
Depression about one or more of the sutures	35	16	3	2
Elevation about coronal suture	2	.. ..	....	....
Parietes very prominent	10	2	....	....
Parietal bosses pointed	1	....	....	....
Occiput very prominent	11	7	....	....
Occiput flattened in some part	3	3	....	....
Occiput irregular	2	....	....	....
Retromastoid region very prominent	1	....	....	....

Abnormalities of the Scalp.

	WHITE		COLORED	
Number of children examined	634	274	66	26
Total number of abnormalities	....	1	......	....
Plexi of veins over	....	1	......	....

Abnormalities of the Hair.

	WHITE.		COLORED	
	Male.	Female.	Male.	Female.
Number of children examined	624	274	66	26
Total number of abnormalities	29	17	1	....
Alopecia (not traceable to disease)	1	....	......	....
Alopecia areata (not traceable to disease)	2	....	......	... ...
Several shades of color	......	1	......	....
Much hair over the forehead	2	1	......	....
Double hair whirl behind	12	12	......	....
Triple whirl behind	......	1	......	....
Hair whirl above the forehead	11	2	1	....
Double whirl above the forehead	1	....	......	....

Abnormalities of the Forehead.

	WHITE.		COLORED	
Number of children examined	634	274	66	26
Total number of abnormalities	41	10	1	... .
Very high	1	1	......	... .
Very low	10	1	......	....
Very narrow	2	....	......	....
Sloping	3	....	......	....
Asymmetrical	16	7	......	....
Square	7	....	......	....
Frontal bosses prominent	2	1	......	....
Prominent in centre	......	....	1	....

Abnormalities of the Face.

	WHITE.		COLORED	
Number of children examined	634	274	66	26
Total number of abnormalities	129	32	15	1
Asymmetrical	50	17	9	....
Smaller on left	12	....	2	....
Smaller on right	6	....	......	....
Very long	......	1	......	....
Esquimaux like	1	....	......	....
Lower part heavy	1	....	......	....
Brows heavy	1	....	......	....
Eyes deep set	1	....	......	....
Eyes unequal in position	......	1	......	....
Eye slits oblique	1	....	......	....
Wall of left orbit irregular	......	1	......	....
Mongolic folds	17	7	......	1
Canthi deficient	1	1	......	....
Right iris double color	......	1	......	....
Nose deflected	7	2	......	....
Nose irregular	2	1	......	....
Nose flat	1	....	......	....
Nose low	11	....	2	....
Nose broad root	8	... ..	2	....
Nose septum low	1	....	......	....
Nose septum deficient	1	....	......	....
Vault of superior maxillary low	1	....	......	....
Left labial angle lower	1	....	......	....
Lips thick	2	....	......	....
Chin pointed	2	....	......	....
Chin receding	1	....	......	....

FIG. 4.— Hair whirl above the forehead; tendency to a double whirl in this case. Anomaly, congenital, causation uncertain.

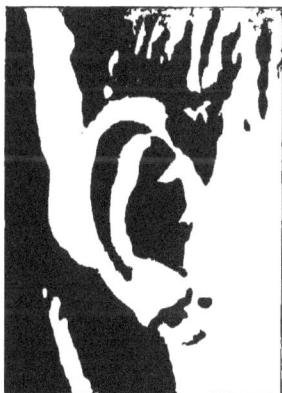

FIG. 5.— Double lobule of right ear. Anomaly, apparently congenital in this case. Due to defect in the development of the part.

FIG. 6. a.—Flaring ears. Anomaly, of congenital origin, causation uncertain.

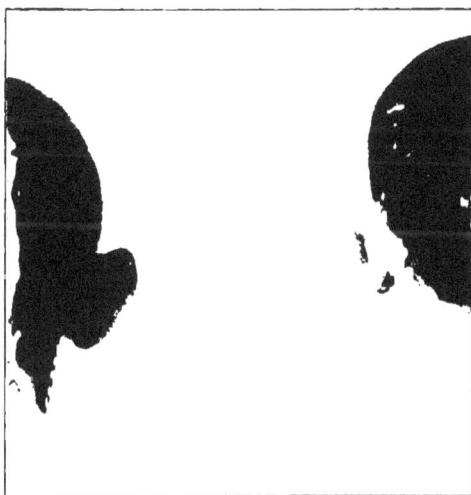

FIG. 6, b.

Abnormalities of the Ears.

	WHITE.		COLORED.	
	Male.	Female.	Male.	Female.
Number of children examined	634	274	66	26
Total number of abnormalities	222	88	20	8
Uneven	2			
Irregular	2			
Right normal, left abnormal	11	2	1	
Left normal, right abnormal	17	6		
Deficient in evolution	3			
Lower part deficient in evolution	2			
Upper one-third deficient in evolution	1			
Thick	3	1		
Flaring	29	1	1	
Upper half flaring	2	1		
Bent on themselves	11	2		
Upper one third bent on itself	1			
Helices deficient	77	54	5	3
deformed	2		6	2
compressed	8	7	1	
overhanging	3	1		1
very thick	1			
Ante helices deficient	28	6		1
irregular	2			
very prominent	1	1		
Lobules deficient	13	5	6	1
heavy	2			
adherent		1		
Right lobule bilobe	1			

Abnormalities of the Gums.

	Male.	Female.	Male.	Female.
Number of children examined	634	274	66	26
Total number of abnormalities	163	67	9	2
Asymmetrical	2			
Defect in middle of both		2		
Massive both	4	2		
Prognathic	14	8		
Upper—				
asymmetrical	3			
irregular	2	1		
prognathic	26	26		
narrow in front	8	4		
V-shaped	1			
massive	87	18	9	2
flat	1			
Lower—				
asymmetrical		1		
polygonal	13	3		
bony prominence		1		
Upper labial frenum low		1		
Mucous membrane adherent	1			

Abnormalities of the Teeth—Dentition.

	Male.	Female.	Male.	Female.
Number of children examined	634	274	66	26
Total number of abnormalities	8	2		
Wanting—				
left bicuspid		1		
lower second incisors	1			
all second incisors	1			
second left incisors	1			
second upper incisors	2			
second left upper and lower incisors	1			
Supernumerary—				
an incisor in both jaws	1			
double teeth in place of lower incisor and canine		1		
Left upper canine double	1			

Abnormalities of the Teeth—Denture.

	WHITE.		COLORED.	
	Male.	Female.	Male.	Female.
Number of children examined	634	274	66	26
Total number of abnormalities	116	48	15	2
Very large	1			
Diminutive	10	4		
Canines very high	11		1	
with tubercles	7	1	6	
Incisors with tubercles	2		1	
Corrugations on teeth	11	3	3	1
Teeth Inverted	4	1		
Incisors irregularly set	26	22	3	
Canines irregularly set	3	3		
Diastema around one or more teeth	41	14	1	1

Abnormalities of the Palate.

Number of children examined	634	274	66	26
Total number of abnormalities	228	114	15	10
Asymmetrical	38	26	2	3
Irregular	1		1	
Broad	1			
Narrow	81	29	4	
High	69	43	3	6
Shallow	1			
High and narrow	7		1	
V-shaped anteriorly	4	1		
Gothic	5	1		
Small	1			
Torus	20	14	4	

Abnormalities of the Uvula.

Number of children examined	634	274	66	26
Total number of abnormalities	129	62	15	4
Deformed	3			
Very long	1		1	1
Very small	4	3		
Biped	7	2		
More posterior than usual	1			
Deflected to left	42	20	7	
Deflected to right	67	25	6	2
Absent	1	1		
Could not be examined on account of excessive sensitiveness	3	2	1	1

Abnormalities of the Limbs.

Number of children examined	634	274	66	26
Total number of abnormalities	95	46	15	5
Hands long	1			
Left upper limb smaller than right	1			1
Right arm smaller than left	1			
Right humerus bent forward	1			
Right limb small and short	2			
Curvature of femur	8	2	5	
Curvature of bones of the leg	1	1	7	2
Legs and feet abnormally short			1	
Limbs below knees uniform in size (not œdema)	1			
Feet very long		1	1	
Fore part of feet very broad	1			

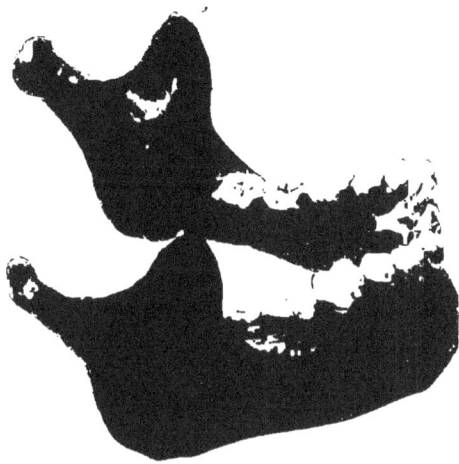

FIG. 7.—Polygonal lower jaw, adult. The teeth do not form an arch, but a figure with three straight sides. Anomaly, probably of congenital origin, though late in development, and accentuated by strong canines. Occurs typically in lower jaw only.

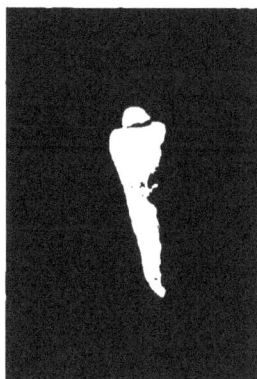

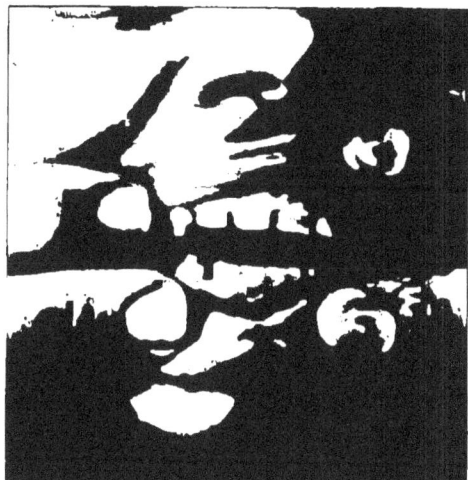

Fig. 8. b.

Fig. 8. a.—Canines surmounted by a tubercle.
Anomaly, acquired, probably of rachitic origin.*

Fig. 9. Teeth showing marked indentations, in rows. Anomaly, acquired, probably
of rachitic origin.

*See Anthropolog. Studies of the Syracuse Feeble-Minded Children, by the author
(Supplemental Report of the Institution, 1898).

Abnormalitics of the Limbs—(Continued).

	WHITE.		COLORED	
	Male.	Female.	Male.	Female.
Toes :				
First toes very long	8	9	......	1
First toes very short	1	....	......	....
Second toe longer than first and third	10	4	.....	....
Second toe shorter than third	1	1	.....	....
Second toe bent outward	1	....	......	....
Second toe overlap third	6	2	......	......
Second toe contracted	1	....	......	....
Second toes point downward and outward	1	....	......	....
Second and third toes longer than first	8	6	1	1
Second and third toes partly joined at base	16	10	1	....
Marked spaces between first and second toes	7	2	......	....
Third toes longer than second and fourth	2	4	......	....
Third toes shorter than second and fourth	1	....	......	....
Third toes contracted	1	....	......	....
Third toes point inward and downward	1	....	......	....
Third and fourth toes diminutive	......	1	......	....
Fourth toe longer than third	1	....	......	....
Fourth and fifth toes much smaller than third	1	1	......	....
Fifth toe very short	1	....	......	....
Depression in heel	......	1	......	....
(Tattooing on limbs)	(10)	....	......	....

Abnormalities of the Body.

	WHITE		COLORED	
	Male.	Female.	Male.	Female.
Number of children examined	634	274	66	26
Total number of abnormalities	133	31	20	6
Frail	2	2	......	....
Anæmic	......	3	......	....
Marasmatic	1	....	......	....
Left side shorter than right	......	1	......	....
Left side stronger than right	1	....	......	....
Lower half of the body strongest (rachitic)	1	....	......	....
Shoulders very sloping	1	....	......	....
right lower	45	6	3	....
left lower	12	2	2	....
right narrow	1	....	......	....
right smaller than left	1	....	......	....
Clavicles bent upwards	2	....	......	....
Supraclavicular space very small	1	....	......	....
Suprasternal depression very large	......	2	......	....
Chest:				
flat	2	2	......	....
prominent on left	....	....	1	....
deformed in front	....	1	......	....
left side larger	4	....	......	....
left side smaller	1	1	......	....
deformed irregularly	1	....	......	....
prominent in middle, or chicken-breasted	20	6	2	1
protruding in a summit	1	....	......	....
left edge of sternum higher	2	....	......	....
receding in centre	1	....	......	....
depression over sternum	3	....	1	....
flattening below clavicles	1	....	......	....
right side of chest flat	1	....	......	....
depression over cartileges below nipples	3	2	......	2
groove below sternum	1	....	......	....
marked prominent hollow over 6th, 7th, 8th and 9th ribs	1	....	......	....
right side of chest narrow	1	....	......	....
double large fatty fold in front of axilla	......	....	......	1
dark spots over chest and abdomen	......	1	1	....
Dorsal spine inclined	5	1	3	2
spinal curvature (permanent)	1	....	1	....
whirl of hair over upper dorsal region	......	1	1	1
Skin pigmented	1	....	......	....

Abnormalities of the Body—(Continued).

	WHITE.		COLORED.	
	Male.	Female.	Male.	Female.
Abdomen :				
umbilical hernia	2	....	3	....
inguinal hernia, left	1	....	......	....
Right hip prominent	3	....	......	....
Buttocks :				
gluteal fold long	1	....	......	....
gluteal fold very short	1	....	......	....
gluteal fold oblique	6	....	......	....
buttocks very prominent	1	....	1	....
gluteal fold inclined to right	......	....	2	....

Abnormalities of the Genitals.

Number of children examined	634	274	66	2
Total number of abnormalities	277	?	27	?
Penis very large	8	....	1	....
very long	1	....	......	....
very short	5	....	......	....
very small	9	....	......	....
Glans small	1	....	......	....
Penis flexed to left	1	....	......	....
Phimoses	32	....	6	....
Prepuce adherent	193	....	16	....
contracted	1	....	......	....
narrow	10	....	1	....
very long and thickened	1	....	1	....
Hypospadiasis	1	....	......	....
Scrotum almost absent	1	....	......	....
Testicles absent.	1	....	......	....
One testicle absent	1	....	1	....
One testicle not descended (but palpable)	6	....	1	....
Both testicles not descended " "	1	....	......	....
Testicles very small	1	....	......	....
relatively large	1	....	......	....
Varicocele on left testicle	1	....	......	....
White spots on base of penis	1	....	......	....

The principal facts which the preceding data reflect are the
following:

The variety of the irregularities observed in the children of the
Juvenile Asylum is very great. There is no *one*, nor any set of the
abnormalities, which runs through such a number of subjects, that
we could consider it typical of the asylum children, or of any similar
class. There is no abnormal *type* of individuals present in the institution: whatever abnormal individuals there may be there are but
exceptions.

A very large proportion of the observed abnormalities is of but
a slight character, and of very little objective or subjective effect on

FIG. 10.—Second and third toes united for about half their length from their base (two subjects). Congenital anomaly, various degrees of which are very common both in children and adults.

the individual. These characters will interfere but very little, if at all, with any progress in life of which the child may be otherwise capable.

In addition to the above data, I have endeavored to pick out and *contrast the different abnormalities according to their origin.* It was found that the majority of the atypical characters can be referred to three classes of origin, that is, either among the inborn, or congenital characters, which are not due to any disease or injury; or among those which were acquired through some pathological process; or among those which were acquired through some habit of the individual.

In about one-third of all the abnormalities the origin was not certain, and all these cases were included in the group which will be marked " Origin questionable." The result of this part of the analysis is shown by the following interesting figures:

The proportion of congenital abnormalities was in the white males as 1.52 to each subject examined, or, approximately, there were three of such abnormalities to each two white boys. Similar proportions in the white females were 1.07 to each individual, or, approximately, one to each child.

In the colored male and female the proportions were respectively 1.03 and 0.73 to each child.

Thus abnormalities of congenital origin are considerably more frequent, in both white and colored males, than they are in the females of the two classes.

Furthermore, congenital abnormalities in both sexes of the white children are considerably more numerous than they are in the corresponding sexes of the colored subjects. The colored children are born more free from physical defects than are the white children.

As to the abnormalities acquired through some pathological process, we obtained the following proportions in the different classes of children.

In the white male there were 0.56 of such acquired character to each child, and about 1 such irregularity in each two individuals.

In white girls the proportion is 0.50 to each child, or exactly 1 to each individual.

In the colored male similar proportion is 0.88 to each individual, which would make approximately two of such abnormalities in every three boys; while in the colored female the number was 0.68 to each child, which would make about three abnormalities to every four children.

The figures just given show that acquired abnormalities through pathological processes are, in opposition to congenital abnormalities, considerably more frequent in the colored children of both sexes than they are in the white.

In both classes of children we again notice a somewhat larger proportion of the irregularities in the male children.

Of abnormalities acquired by habit the white males show 0.125 to each person, or 1 to 8 individuals; the white female children 0.04, or about 1 in 26 individuals. In the colored children similar proportions were respectively 0.16 in the boys and 0.10. to each child in the girls, or about 1 to 6 in the male and 1 to 9 in the female individuals.

In both white and colored children, abnormalities acquired by habit are seen to be more frequent in the boys than they are in the girls, and in the negro children of both sexes the proportion of these characters preponderates over that found in the white children.

The characters whose origin is questionable are found in almost equal proportions in the different classes of children; there are about 2 of such characters to 3 children, excepting the colored boys, where the proportion was found only about 1 in 2 individuals.

To sum up in a few words the results of the data just given, we find that on an average all classes of abnormalities predominate in the male children, both white and colored. This predominance is especially marked in the case of the irregularities acquired by habit.

The white and colored children differ in their abnormalities very remarkably. The white children of both sexes possess on an average a decidedly larger proportion of inborn abnormalities. On the other hand, the negro children acquire in early life a larger percentage of irregularities than the white children. These facts signify that while the white children are more likely to be begotten with physical deficiencies, yet later in life they will not undergo so many pathological processes which give rise to physical abnormalities, as will the negro children. Rachitis seems to be particularly more frequent in the colored.

A large number of the lighter congenital abnormalities in no way reflects badly on the individual's history, and does not show any predispositions of the child. Science has been as yet unable to trace to their real causes such atypical characters or irregularities as those of the ears, or those of the toes, or some of those of the teeth, the palate or the uvula; and experience teaches plentifully that there is but very little or no practical significance to these characters.

The sum total of my observations on the abnormalities of the inmates of the New York Juvenile Asylum leads me to conclude, as before stated, that we have here to deal with a class of children, the large majority of whom, so far as physical abnormalities are concerned, are fairly average individuals.

There are many irregularities in the children which are due to neglect and can and ought to be corrected.

A small proportion of the inmates apparently are the children of unhealthy parents, as a result of which descendance they have fallen subject to states of malnutrition or to rachitis, which conditions left them with numerous physical abnormalities.

I found no single child, whom I could conscientiously term a thorough physical degenerate.

To conclude this subject I will give here a table illustrating the proportions of congenital and acquired abnormalities according to the different parts of the body.

Total of Abnormalities—White Males.

	Congenital.	Acquired as a result of some pathol. process.	Acquired by habit.	Cause of acquisition uncertain.
Head		74		15
Scalp				
Hair	26	2		1
Forehead	15	25		1
Face	51	68		10
Eyes				15
Ears	221			
Teeth	67	20		37
Gums	51	7		104
Palate	88	59		81
Uvula	14			112
Body	5	54	72	2
Limbs	60	14		11
Genitals	275	1		1
Totals	873	324	72	390
Percentages	40	10	4	18
Proportion to each child with abnormalities	1.52	.56	.12	.67

Total of Abnormalities—White Females.

	Congenital.	Acquired as a result of some pathol. process.	Acquired by habit.	Cause of acquisition uncertain.
Head		26		10
Scalp	1			
Hair	17			
Forehead	1	8		1
Face	11	17		4
Eyes				6
Ears	88			
Teeth	19	4		27
Gums	41	3		23
Palate	30	40		44
Uvula	6			54
Body	3	18	9	1
Limbs	39	4		3
Genitals				
Totals	256	120	9	173
Percentages	45	21	1	30
Proportion to each child with abnormalities	1.07	.50	.003	.71

Total of Abnormalities—Colored Males.

	Congenital.	Acquired as a result of some pathol. process.	Acquired by habit.	Cause of acquisition uncertain
Head		5		
Forehead		1		
Hair	1			
Face	4	11		
Ears	20			
Teeth	2	10		3
Gums				10
Palate	4	7		4
Uvula	1			13
Body	1	8	10	1
Limbs	3	12		
Genitals	27			
Totals	63	54	10	31
Percentages	39	34	6	19
Proportion to each child with abnormalities	1.03	.88	.16	.50

Total of Abnormalities—Colored Females.

	Congenital.	Acquired as a result of some pathol. process.	Acquired by habit.	Cause of acquisition uncertain.
Head		2		
Forehead				
Hair				
Face	1			
Ears	8			
Teeth	1	1		4
Gums				4
Palate		4		6
Uvula	1			2
Body	1	3	2	
Limbs	2	3		
Genitals				
Totals	14	13	2	12
Percentages	34	31	4	29
Proportion to each child with abnormalities	.73	.68	.10	.63

Lungs and Heart.

It will be well to add in this place the results of the examination of the thoracic organs in the children.

It was rather a surprise to me not to find among the whole 1,000 children more than one case in which it could be positively said that there existed a consolidation in some parts of the lungs. This case was that of a small negro boy, who has since left the asylum; he had a consolidation of both apices. There were perhaps a dozen additional cases in which percussion sounds over the apices were not as clear as they ought to be, but there were no râles audible, nor were there present any other signs of a lung trouble in these individuals.

Notwithstanding the encouraging results of the examination of the lungs of the inmates of the asylum, it is undoubtedly a fact that a certain percentage of these children carry a predisposition to consumption, and require additional care.

The heart was found to be entirely normal in 955 cases out of the 1,000 children examined. In 10 other cases the disturbance of the organ was light and might have been but temporary. In the remaining cases the disorders found were as follows:

	WHITE.		COLORED.	
	Male.	Female.	Male.	Female.
Heart action abnormally rapid	2	....	......	....
Heart very slow (strong)	1	....	......	....
Heart very feeble	1	....	......	....
Heart action persistently irregular	7	4	......	1
Systolic murmur	11	....	1	....
Decided mitral insufficiency	1	....	......	....
Cardiac hypertrophy	2	3	......	....

The colored children, as the preceding figures show, are much more free from cardiac disorders than are the white children.

The disorders observed are undoubtedly, in the majority of the cases, due to such conditions as general anaemia or neurasthenia, and will disappear with the cure of the latter.

Of the few organic disorders of the heart, no one was of a congenital origin.

The proportion of disorders of the heart in the asylum children, as expressed by the above figures, cannot be considered unusual.

Left-Handedness.

In addition to the preceding examinations an effort was made to ascertain the number of left-handed individuals among the children. There is no particular significance in the simple fact that a person is left-handed, or at least we know as yet positively of no such significance, and the investigations as to this point have up to now been largely only statistical.

Among the 1,000 inmates of the asylum there were 6 left-handed boys and 4 left-handed girls. In some of these subjects the left-handedness probably is more apparent than real as, in 2 of the boys and 3 of the girls, notwithstanding the left-handedness, the right arm was found to be the stronger.

Measurements of the Children.

The measurements of the children differ largely according to age and hence they cannot be treated of fully before we approach the second part of the report. The only facts which I can bring forth advantageously in this place are a few notes on the shapes of the heads, in several of the larger groups of children of different nationalities. I will introduce these variations in the form of curves which will show the various percentages of the different shapes of heads in the different groups, but before I will give the curves. I think it advisable to say a few words of explanation on the subject.

It has been found after extensive studies, mainly in France, England and Germany, that the shape of the head differs quite remarkably, not only between people of different color, but also among families of the white race, and that these differences within certain limits are quite stable with each such family. The shape of the head is determined principally by three measurements, namely the maximum length, the maximum width and the height of the cranium. The percentage derived by dividing the width by the length of the head gives us what we call the *cephalic index*, which is a true expression of the shape of the horizontal plane of the head. The lower the figure of this cephalic index the more the skull approaches the shape of an oval, the higher the index the more the head is round. In a general way all heads up to the index of 75 are termed long, skulls from 75 up to 80 medium, and skulls above 80 short. This explanation I think will add to the interest of the following curves with those who have not had the opportunity to give special attention to anthropometry.

A glance over the curves shows that the shape of the head presents in most of the white families here shown a considerable variation. This variation bespeaks a far advanced mixture of the families. In the Irish, the Italian and the German such mixture dates from centuries ago and may even reach to prehistoric times. Thus the Irish people of to-day result from the mixture of the ancient inhabitants of Erin with the short-headed Kelt and the long-headed Scotchman. The Germans of to-day are a combination of old long-headed Teutonic tribes and of the short-headed Slav and Kelt. The Italians are principally a mixture of Romans and Greeks, of short-headed Lydians, and of long-headed Teutonic branches. The variety in the shape of the head among the American children is a result of the mixture of almost all the human families, members of which immigrated here, and is taking place at the present epoch.

The heads of the Russian and those of the Syrian children are quite uniform, and these families of the white race are undoubtedly purer than are any of those mentioned above. It ought to be remarked that the Russian children here represented were all except one, Jews.

The colored children show a large proportion of long heads. Most of the subjects with the shorter heads are not of African descent, but from the West Indies.

PART II.

DETAILED STUDY.

This part of the report could be made very extensive, but I will restrict it to the most salient facts. Of necessity, I will have to introduce here a number of tables of figures.

Inspection.

I have not much additional to say here about the abnormalities found in the children. The following table will show the proportions of abnormalities to the number of children found to present some abnormality according to their different ages.

White Children.

AGE.	NUMBER EXAMINED.		ENTIRELY NORMAL.		CHILDREN WITH ABNORMALITIES.		PROPORTION OF ABNORMALITIES TO NUMBER OF CHILDREN.	
	Male.	Female.	Male.	Female.	Male.	Female.	Male.	Female.
5............	2	2	1	....	1	2	1.00	4.00
6............	15	10	....	....	15	10	2.93	2.00
7............	38	34	....	3	38	31	2.82	2.26
8............	56	42	3	5	53	37	3.15	2.41
9............	62	45	4	8	58	37	3.31	2.59
10............	98	52	16	7	82	45	2.80	2.11
11............	99	40	5	9	94	31	2.57	2.19
12............	93	14	9	....	84	14	2.78	2.21
13............	86	10	10	2	76	17	2.88	2.35
14	53	10	7	1	46	9	2.78	2.89
15............	20	4	3	....	17	4	2.88	2.50
16............	9	1	....	....	9	1	(3.22)	(3.00)
17............	3	....	....	....	3	....	(3.67)	....
18............	....	1	....	....	....	1	....	(2.00)
	634	274	58	35	576	239	2.71	2.33

Colored Children.

AGE.	NUMBER EXAMINED.		ENTIRELY NORMAL.		CHILDREN WITH ABNORMALITIES.		PROPORTION OF ABNORMALITIES TO NUMBER OF CHILDREN.	
	Male.	Female.	Male.	Female.	Male.	Female.	Male.	Female.
5	....	......	....	....	....	....	....	....
6	1	....	....	....	1	....	(2.00)	....
7	1	4	....	1	1	3	(3.00)	(2.00)
8	5	1	1	....	4	1	(3.00)	(3.00)
9	12	5	1	2	11	3	2.64	(1.67)
10	6	2	....	....	6	2	2.50	(2.00)
11	7	6	1	2	6	4	1.17	(2.50)
12	7	3	....	....	7	3	2.70	(1.67)
13	12	1	2	....	10	1	2.60	(2.00)
14	7	2	....	2	7	....	3.14	....
15	6	2	....	....	6	2	3.17	(3.00)
16	2	....	....	....	2	....	(2.00)	....
17	....	....	....	....	....	....	....	....
18	....	....	....	....	....	....	....	....
	66	26	5	7	61	19	2.60	2.05

The proportions, it can be seen, show no very great variations. The maximum of abnormalities is encountered in children of both sexes at the ages of 8 and 9. In the female another maximum was observed at 14, but this latter is in all probability an incorrect figure, due to a small number of subjects involved. After 9 years of age the proportion of abnormalities to every child drops suddenly and further on shows only insignificant variations.

We do not encounter the same proportions of the same abnormalities in the children of different ages. In the younger children there will predominate abnormalities of the teeth, of the gums, of the face and of the lower limbs. The younger the child is, the more frequently we find irregularities in dentition, massive gums, mongolic folds at the inner corners of the eyes, low nose, and curvatures of the lower limbs. Curvatures of the long bones will diminish with the age of the children and may finally almost disappear.

Mongolic folds at the inner canthi of the eyes are very much more common in infants than they are in children above 6 years of age, and eventually they also will disappear, except in a few female subjects where they may persist throughout life. Massive gums are the normal condition in very early childhood. After 8 years of age, and probably a little sooner, they can be considered abnormalities. As we go on with the age of the children, massive gums become less and less frequent, and after the puberty period they are among the rare abnormalities. The nose, which may be very low, or very broad at the root in very early age, will gradually assume ordinary proportions and lose its abnormal aspect, as the child grows up.

On the other hand, certain abnormalities will increase in frequency with the age of the children. Such is the case principally with many of the abnormalities of the cranium, such as asymmetries of the head and depressions or elevations along the sutures. Asymmetries of the face are generally well defined during childhood, and I am not satisfied whether or not there is any increase in their proportion with the age. Abnormalities of the ears become more marked and also increase somewhat in proportion from infancy onward. All the habit abnormalities tend to increase in proportion as we advance from early childhood. From my observations of adults and adolescents outside of the Institution, I think that after the age of 15 or 16, these abnormalities tend again to diminish, a certain proportion of them being spontaneously corrected. Irregularities of the palate increase with age. About those of the uvula I am uncertain though they also seem to increase in frequency with age. Certain abnormal gums do not become manifest until after the subject has reached a certain age. Such is principally the polygonal gum. Prognathism of the gums is also not marked in early childhood; it begins to show from the fourth year of childhood onward, not attaining its ultimate degree until adult life.

The genital organs deserve special mention. Certain abnormalities of these organs in the male, principally adhesions of the prepuce, diminish very rapidly after the puberty period. Other irregularities, principally those of the size of the organs, become more manifest as the child grows older. The descent of the testicles will be occasionally found to be retarded in young boys; it will generally be accomplished before the age of puberty. In connection with this a care should be taken not to mistake testicles reflexly drawn up for non-descended testicles.

A certain number of abnormalities, almost all of which are of congenital origin, do not change in proportion with the age of the children. Such characters are the different abnormalities of the toes, the additional whirls of hair, etc. Almost all of these characters, however, become better differenciated and more pronounced with the age of their bearers.

I append here a table which gives the percentages of congenital and other classes of the abnormalities of the children according to their ages. The table suffers very much by the small numbers of individuals represented in some of the divisions; but it shows fairly well the gradual diminution with age of the bulk of congenital defects; the increase with age of the habit abnormalities; and the excess of the congenital defects in the male over the female. The proportions of abnormalities which I included under " origin questionable " increases much with the ages of the children: this increase signifies that some of the characters whose origin I class as questionable are really acquired. There were included in this class of abnormalities, principally, the very prominent occiput; the deflections of the nose; the polygonal gums; most of the abnormalities of the dentition and of the teeth; the high and the gothic palate, and the deflected uvula.

Percentages of abnormalities according to their origin at different ages of the white and colored children, male and female.

AGE.	WHITE MALE.				WHITE FEMALE.				COLORED MALE.				COLORED FEMALE.			
	C	Ap	Ah	?	C.	Ap.	Ah	?	C.	Ap.	Ah.	?	C.	Ap.	Ah.	?
6	58	29	..	11	52	21	..	21	33	33	..	33	..	..	..	..
7	55	24	8	12	45	24	..	29	..	50	..	50	20	40	..	40
8	52	17	3	27	48	17	..	32	50	33	..	16	..	50	50	..
9	60	15	3	22	31	34	..	34	39	32	..	28	33	..	..	66
10	55	12	4	23	43	23	3	30	31	43	..	18	66	..	..	33
11	51	22	4	23	51	12	..	32	16	50	16	16	30	50	..	20
12	54	17	30	25	54	25	..	19	61	22	..	11	40	40	20	..
13	49	20	6	24	52	10	..	34	46	26	7	19	..	..	..	..
14	48	22	6	21	42	19	..	38	36	22	13	27	..	..	..	..
15	46	24	9	24	..	..	..	..	21	57	10	10	..	..	..	..
16	44	18	11	37	..	..	..	..	..	..	..	..	..	..	..	..

C.=congenital.   Ap.=acquired as a result of some pathological process.   Ah.=acquired through habit.   ?=origin uncertain.

Measures.

The results of the measuring when tabulated according to the ages of the children proved to be of great interest, and the facts that some of these tabulations clearly show are new. Some disturbance in the figures was occasioned throughout by the small numbers of subjects in some of the divisions, but these irregularities are apparent and do not affect the rules which the different columns of figures demonstrate. I was further afraid that the numerous nationalities of the children may prove a disturbing element in the total results. Such disturbance, however, was noticed only in the crude figures; the relations of the different data obtained remained practically the same, whether only one group or all of the white children were considered. I will here give each of the measurements taken on the children arranged in a comprehensive table adding only such remarks to each division as I think necessary or advisable.

Height of the Children.

The group figures of this measure are much more than any other affected by the nationality of the children. There is in the asylum a very large number of Italian children, and these are generally much smaller than are the American-born subjects. The Russian children are also considerably smaller. In consequence the average height of all the children taken together will not represent figures fit to be compared with any figures obtained on subjects of a more homogeneous nature. The value of the figures showing the average height of the children of the Juvenile Asylum consists principally in their being a basis for comparison with other measurements of the same individuals. With the colored males and colored females the figures given have a fuller value.

Height.

AGE.	WHITE MALES.		WHITE FEMALES.		COLORED MALES.		COLORED FEMALES.	
	Number examined.	Average height	Number examined.	Average height.	Number examined.	Average height.	Number examined	Average height.
3	......	....	......	....	1	783mm.	2	839
4	......	....	......	....	......	....	2	906
5	2	961mm.	2	1004mm.	3	1044	4	985
6	15	1051	10	1069	5	1101	2	1091
7	38	1120	34	1086	5	1147	9	1127
8	56	1152	42	1130	13	1196	5	1260
9	62	1212	45	1187	25	1251	10	1257
10	98	1248	52	1267	12	1271	8	1295
11	99	1315	40	1304	12	1360	9	1307
12	93	1362	14	1357	10	1381	3	1467
13	86	1420	19	1431	13	1392	1	1477
14	53	1449	16	1495	7	1505	2	1559
15	20	1462	4	1535	6	1455	2	1545
16	9	1615	1	1498	2	1500	......	....
17	3	1654	......	....	......	....	......	....
18	......	....	1	1554	......	....	......	....

I have extracted the heights of children born in this country and
of American parentage and will give next the measurements of the
height of these children and, for a comparison, the heights of Boston
school children who were born in this country.*

Height of American-born Children—Males.

(1) Asylum children.   (2) Boston school children

	5 years.	6 years.	7 years.	8 years.	9 years.	10 years.	11 years.	12 years	13 years.	14 years.	15 years.	16 years.
(1)	971	1088	1172	1163	1234	1261	1315	1367	1424	1452	1518	1697
(2)	1060	1120	1174	1223	1272	1326	1372	1417	1477	1551	1599	1665

Females.

	5 years.	6 years.	7 years.	8 years.	9 years.	10 years.	11 years.	12 years	13 years.	14 years.	15 years.	16 years.
(1)	.....	.....	1101	1158	1204	1289	1290	1454	1450	1398	....	.....
(2)	1053	1109	1167	1221	1260	1315	1366	1452	1492	1532	1559	1567

The preceding table shows that the American-born children in the
Juvenile Asylum are on an average somewhat smaller at almost all
the ages than the free children of American parentage from the
schools of Boston. The comparison, however, is not fully satisfac-
tory. We ought to have a row of figures showing the height of the
American-born children of New York City instead of Boston.
The Boston population is principally composed of Americans and
Germans. A great many of the American people of Boston are of
English or German descent, and people of both these nationalities
are above the average in stature. The American-born population of
New York is composed principally of the German and Irish ele-
ments, but besides this there enters into it a large percentage of
Hebrews, principally of Russian or Polish origin; of Italians and
of people of other nationalities, and the average height of many of
these people is low. Thus it may be expected that the New York-
born American children would show a somewhat smaller average
stature than the children born in Boston. This point cannot, however, be here decided. The inmates of the Juvenile Asylum are on
an average undoubtedly of a somewhat subnormal height. It cannot
be otherwise upon pure physiological laws, with children who come
from the poorest classes of the population. A similar fact was found

* "Massachusetts School Children," by Dr. H. P. Powditch, Mass. St. Board of Health
publication, 1877, 1890.

by Dr. Franz Boas, who some years ago examined with Dr. West numerous school children in Worcester, Mass. Dr. Boas informed me that he found the children of poorer families to be on the average perceptibly smaller than the children of well to do people. The heights of Italian children, which follow, will be seen to be considerably below the heights of not only the children of American parentage, but also ,below the average heights of all the children together in the institution. I have no data at hand by which I could show whether these Italian children are below the average in stature of Italian children outside the asylum. If we should compare these figures with figures obtained from Italian children in the city of New York, we would hardly find great differences, as most of the Italians here are poor people.

Height—Italian Children.

	6 years.	7 years.	8 years.	9 years.	10 years.	11 years.	12 years.	13 years.	14 years.	15 years.
Males......	1025	1113	1134	1197	1234	1287	1337	1368	1226	1357
Females ...	1058	1081	1109	1155	1246	1290	1336	1370	1483	....

Sitting Height.

Tables 4 and 5 will show the sitting height as obtained on the children of the institution, and the proportions of the sitting height, or of the length of the lower extremities, to the total height of the body. The interest lies principally in these latter named proportions. A glance at the figures will show that in both the white and the negro children of small age the proportion of the length of the lower limbs to the total height of the body is comparatively small, and that it increases with considerable precision and regularity during all the years up to and possibly even beyond the age of puberty. This means that as a child advances in life its limbs are growing in proportion somewhat more rapidly than its body. In a new born infant the lower limbs are very short. The greatest length of the lower limbs seems to be attained from the thirteenth to sixteenth years of an individual. I have myself but a very few data on children older than 16, but from Dr. West's report* on the Worcester school chil-

---

* Gerald Montgomery West, Arch. of Anthropol., XXII., p. 13 et seq.; in this connection also Boas, The Growth of Children, Science, April 9, '97.

dren in Massachusetts, it would appear that after 15 or 16 years of age the greater proportion of growth of the lower limbs ceases and that from then onward, up to the end of the growing period, the body seems to increase slightly in proportion to the lower extremities.

An interesting feature which can be observed in the above figures is the greater proportionate length, by an average of about 1 per cent., of the total body height of the lower limbs in the negro children.

When I compare my sitting height indexes with similar indexes obtained by Dr. West, it appears that the indexes of Dr. West's children were at all ages somewhat smaller or that the lower extremities in these children were at all ages somewhat longer than they are in our children in the asylum. The difference amounts on an average to from 1 to 1.5 per cent of the body height. These figures make me think that it is possible that it is in the lower extremities where lies the principal defect in the growth of the badly nourished children; but I can say nothing positive on this point. Similar differences exist, I have some reason to believe, between free, well nourished, and asylum colored children.

Sitting Height.

AGE.	WHITE MALES.		WHITE FEMALES.		COLORED MALES.		COLORED FEMALES.	
	Average sitting height.	Average height of lower limbs.	Average sitting height.	Average height of lower limbs.	Average sitting height.	Average height of lower limbs.	Average sitting height.	Average height of lower limbs.
	cm.	cm.	cm.	cm.	cm.	cm.	cm.	cm.
3	....	....	....	....	476	307	476	363
4	....	....	....	....	....	....	534	372
5	551	410	576	428	597	447	571	414
6	595	456	608	452	616	485	607	484
7	631	489	621	467	630	517	625	502
8	644	508	645	495	659	537	671	589
9	672	540	663	524	679	572	680	577
10	684	564	687	580	697	574	695	600
11	711	604	718	586	718	642	703	594
12	728	644	734	633	797	584	792	675
13	751	669	770	661	737	655	767	710
14	764	685	809	686	787	718	808	751
15	777	685	825	710	753	692	819	726
16	839	776	824	674	795	705	....	....
17	864	790	850	704	....	....	....	....
18	....	....	....	....	....	....	....	....

Proportions of Sitting Height to Height.

AGE.	WHITE MALES. Average index or percent of sitting height.	WHITE MALES. Average index or percent of height of lower extremities.	WHITE FEMALES. Average index or percent of sitting height.	WHITE FEMALES. Average index or percent of height of lower extremities.	COLORED MALES. Average index or percent of sitting height.	COLORED MALES. Average index or percent of height of lower extremities.	COLORED FEMALES. Average index or percent of sitting height.	COLORED FEMALES. Average index or percent of height of lower extremities.
3.....					60.8	39 2	59.5	40.5
4.....							58 9	41.1
5.....	57.4	42.6	57.3	42.7	57.3	42.7	57.9	42.1
6.....	56.6	43.4	57.4	42.6	55.9	44 1	55 6	44.4
7.....	56.3	43.7	57.2	42.8	54.9	45.1	55.4	44.6
8.....	55.9	44 1	56.2	43.8	55.1	44.9	53.3	46.7
9.....	55.2	44.7	55.9	44.1	54.2	45.8	54.1	45.9
10.....	54.6	45 4	54.2	44.8	54.9	.45.1	53.7	46.3
11.....	54.0	46.0	55.0	45.0	52.8	47.2	53.8	46.2
12.....	53.5	46.5	54.1	45.9	57.7	47 3	54.0	46.0
13.....	52 9	47.1	53.8	46.2	52 9	47.1	51.9	48.1
14.....	52.7	47.3	54.1	45.9	52.3	47.7	51.8	48 2
15.....	53.1	46.9	53.7	46.3	51.7	48 3	53.0	47.0
16.....	52 0	48.0	55.0	45.0	53 0	47.0		
17.....	52.2	47.8	54.7	45 3				

The proportions of sitting height to total body height can be illustrated to further advantage when we cease to consider the ages of the children and consider simply the stature. I give here two tables which will show the sitting height index in its relation to every increase of 50mm. in stature. It will be seen that the relation is quite regular, and also that the greater length of the lower extremities in the colored children is equally true and even more pronounced when we view the matter from this standpoint. I believe that to consider this matter in this way is more important than to consider the relation of sitting height to height simply on the basis of the ages of the children, as we have done above, and as was generally done before by other observers. If similar proportions were ascertained on large numbers of children and in different locations, the data might prove not only of a physiological, but possibly also of forsenic value. The maximum variation of the sitting height index at any age was found not to exceed 8 points.

Relations of Height to Height-Sitting Height Index.

HEIGHT IN MM.	WHITE MALES.		WHITE FEMALES.		COLORED MALES.		COLORED FEMALES.	
	Number of subjects included.	Average corresponding index.	Number of subjects included.	Average corresponding index.	Number of subjects included.	Average corresponding index.	Number of subjects included.	Average corresponding index.
750 to 800....					1	60.8	1	59.9
800 to 850....							1	59.1
850 to 900....							1	58.9
900 to 950....							2	59.05
950 to 1000....	3	57.7	6	57.7	1	59.0	1	58.4
1000 to 1050....	17	57.4	12	57.9	4	57.6	5	55.6
1050 to 1100....	29	56.2	37	56.9	2	55.8	2	55.0
1100 to 1150....	39	56.7	32	56.8	11	55.2	4	56.1
1150 to 1200 ..	62	55.9	27	55.9	8	55.0	7	54.9
1200 to 1250....	73	55.4	48	55.3	12	54.2	6	53.9
1250 to 1300....	78	54.5	22	55.0	16	54.9	9	53.7
1300 to 1350....	105	53.9	29	54.6	16	53.4	12	53.4
1350 to 1400....	74	53.6	24	54.4	17	52.9	8	52.1
1400 to 1450....	66	53.3	12	53.6	11	52 4	1	53.4
1450 to 1500....	44	52.8	11	54.1	8	52.4	2	53.6
1500 to 1550....	18	52.1	10	51 9	4	52.4	3	52.7
1550 to 1600....	11	52.1	4	53.2	3	51.2	2	52.9
1600 to 1650....	8	52.0	1	52.7			1	50.9
1650 to 1700....	4	51.8						
1700 to 1750....	2	51.5						
1750 to 1800 ...								
1800 to 1850....	1	50.0						

Weight.

All the children were weighed in their undergarments and subsequently the weight of these was subtracted from the total weight of the subject. In consequence our figures show the absolute weight of the children and the data are more correct than similar data obtained from children weighed in all their clothing.

The weight in children does not bear a constant relation to the height, and is much more equal in children of different nationalities than is the height measure. I place next to the averages of weight obtained on all the children the averages, first, of American-born children, and second, those of Italians. We will find no such great differences in the two classes of children as we found with the height.

Weight.

AGE.	AVERAGE WEIGHTS.		WEIGHTS OF AMERICAN BORN.		WEIGHTS OF ITALIANS.	
	Male.	Female.	Male.	Female.	Male.	Female.
5	33	34	33	....	....	....
6	40	40	41.8	....	38.8	39
7	45	42	46.8	43.7	44.7	41.3
8	47	45	46.5	46	46.2	43
9	53	52	52	54	53	51
10	57	60	57.1	61.2	56.3	57.5
11	64	65	64	60	61.8	65.3
12	70	72	70	81	68.9	72.1
13	81	84	77.6	74	72	79
14	84	97	81.7	72	85	102
15	85	112	96	....	76	....
16	115	114	140	....	....	....
17	122	....	....	....	....	....
18	....	104	....	....	....	....

If we desire to compare the weight of the inmates of the Juvenile Asylum with weight of children outside of the institution we have again the data collected in Boston from school children by Dr. Bowditch and those collected in Worcester by Drs. West and Boas. In both of these cases the weights are quite similar and hence only one need be stated for comparison. In both cases, however, the children were weighed in their clothing, which, according to Bowditch, whose figures we will state, amounted in average to 7.99 per cent. of the total weight in the boys and 6.81 per cent. of the total weight in the girls. If we should reduce these percentages of pounds from the weight of the Boston school children we should find that the weight was much nearer to the average weight of the children in the Juvenile Asylum. Nevertheless it would still be somewhat greater. The excess is undoubtedly due to the same causes to which was due the smaller stature in the asylum children, namely, to mal-nutrition resulting from the poverty of the parents of the children.

Weight—Males.*

(1) Average weight of asylum children.   (2) Average weight of Boston school children.†

	5 years.	6 years.	7 years.	8 years.	9 years.	10 years	11 years.	12 years.	13 years.	14 years.	15 years.	16 years.	17 years.
(1)	33	40	45	47	53	57	64	70	81	84	85	115	122
(2)	41.9	45.17	49.07	53.9	59.2	65.3	70.18	76.9	84.84	94.91	107.10	121	127.49

* All nationalities.   † Weight of clothing not deducted.

Weight—Females.[*]

(1) Average weight of asylum children.   (2) Average weight of Boston school children.[†]

5 years.	6 years.	7 years.	8 years.	9 years.	10 years.	11 years.	12 years.	13 years.	14 years.	15 years.	16 years.
(1) 34	40	42	45	52	60	65	72	84	97	112	114
(2) 39.6	43.3	47.4	52	57	62.3	68.8	78.3	88.6	98.4	106	112

The average weight of the negro children in the asylum was found to be at most ages slightly smaller than was the average weight of white children. How far this fact is correct in general could only be ascertained by much additional investigation. The fact is that white children, particularly white girls, show, at least up to the age of puberty, more adipose tissue over their body than do the colored children.

Pressure and Traction Force.

In connection with the weight I investigated the force of the hands and arms of the children, so far as this can be ascertained by a correct dynamometer. I have tested the pressure in each hand, as well as the traction force of both arms together, taking as usual only the average of three measurements for the records. As the force was found to differ slightly according to the time of the day at which tested, all of the tests were made at similar hours, that is, in the afternoon.

The figures which I give below show first of all, that average traction force in the children is always considerably smaller than is the pressure force in either hand.

In the second place we see the pressure force in the right hand to be at most ages greater than is the pressure force of the left hand. In individuals there are numerous exceptions to this rule. We find many children in whom the pressure force is either equal in both hands, or is even greater in the left than in the right. The greater pressure force in the left hand was not observed to be associated with left-handedness of the child, except in a few instances. About half of the number of left-handed children on the other hand, were

---

* All nationalities. † Weight of clothing not deducted.

stronger in the right hand. Left-handedness is apparently more a nervous phenomenon than muscular.

In the third place we notice an almost regular annual increase in the force of the children. This is particularly the case in the white male children, where the average annual increase in pressure force amounts to about 4 pounds. The traction force increases only about 2 pounds annually, and the disproportion between the pressure and traction forces of the child grows with the age of the individual.

In the negroes, both the pressure and traction force were found to exceed at all ages similar forces in the white children. This is the more remarkable as we saw that the average weight of the colored subject was at almost all ages less than that of the white children in the asylum. The fact speaks for a greater proportionate muscularity of the colored subjects; this condition was well appreciable during the inspection of the children.

Average Pressure Force in Right Hand of the Children, According to the Color, Sexes and Ages.

AGE.	WHITE.		COLORED.	
	Male.	Female.	Male.	Female.
5	10	8	....	....
6	14	14	16	....
7	18	12	22	12
8	20	16	22	14
9	24	18	26	28
10	28	24	30	24
11	32	26	32	32
12	36	32	44	40
13	40	36	38	44
14	44	42	54	42
15	48	44	50	50
16	68	50	53	....
17	74	....	....	....
18	....	42	....	....

Average Pressure Force in Left Hand of the Children, According to Color, Ages and Sexes.

AGE.	WHITE.		COLORED.	
	Male.	Female.	Male.	Female.
5	10	6	....	....
6	12	14	12	....
7	16	12	20	12
8	18	16	22	12
9	24	16	26	26
10	26	22	28	22
11	30	24	32	26
12	34	32	40	38
13	38	32	36	42
14	40	40	50	40
15	46	42	45	48
16	64	50	48	....
17	72	....	....	....
18	....	38	....	....

Average Traction Force of the Children, According to Color, Sexes and Ages.

AGE.	WHITE.		COLORED.	
	Male.	Female.	Male.	Female.
5	6	4	....	....
6	10	10	8	....
7	12	10	14	8
8	14	10	14	8
9	18	12	18	16
10	20	16	22	16
11	24	18	24	20
12	24	20	28	20
13	28	22	26	30
14	28	26	36	24
15	32	24	31	34
16	44	22	30	....
17	40	....	....	....
18	....	30	....	....

The pressure and traction powers can be studied a point further. We can study the relations of these items to the weight of the children. The next table will show such relations in both the white and colored children grouped together. The figures show that the younger the child is, the smaller is its proportionate force in pounds to each pound of the weight of its body. Curiously, there is a distinct and persistent annual increase in this proportion, and when we reach the seventeenth year of life we find that the proportion of muscular power in the hands and arms of the individual to his body-weight has about doubled.

With the colored individuals we observe the interesting fact that at almost all ages there exists in these children a greater proportionate strength to each pound of the body than is the case with the white children.

The relations of force to weight here exposed may give rise to much speculation as to their real causes.

Relations of Pressure and Traction Force, in Pounds, to Each Pound of Weight, in Children of the Different Color and Sexes, and According to Age.

AGE.	PRESSURE FORCE ON RIGHT HAND, RELATION IN POUNDS TO EACH POUND OF WEIGHT.				PRESSURE FORCE ON LEFT HAND, RELATION IN POUNDS TO EACH POUND OF WEIGHT.				TRACTION FORCE, RELATION IN POUNDS TO EACH POUND OF WEIGHT.			
	White male.	White female.	Colored male.	Colored female.	White male.	White female.	Colored male.	Colored female.	White male.	White female.	Colored male.	Colored female.
5	0.30	0.23	....	....	0.30	0.18	....	....	0.18	0.12	....	....
6	0.35	0.35	0.44	....	0.30	0.35	0.33	....	0.25	0.25	0.22	....
7	0.40	0 29	0.53	0.31	0 36	0.29	0.49	0.31	0.24	0.23	0.34	0.21
8	0.42	0.36	0.45	0.35	0.38	0.36	0 45	0.30	0.30	9.22	0.29	0.20
9	0.45	0.35	0.50	0.47	0.45	0.31	0.50	0.44	0.34	0.23	0.35	0.27
10	0.49	0.40	0.51	0.40	0.46	0.37	0.47	0.37	0.35	0.27	0.37	0.27
11	0.50	0.40	0.50	0.53	0.47	0.37	0.50	0.43	0.37	0.27	0.37	0.33
12	0.51	0.44	0.63	0.37	0.49	0.44	0.57	0.36	0.34	0.28	0.40	0.19
13	0.50	0.43	0.55	0.47	0.47	0.38	0.49	0.45	0.34	0.26	0.36	0.32
14	0.52	0.43	0.57	0.42	0.48	0.41	0.53	0.40	0.33	0.27	0.38	0.24
15	0.56	0.39	0.61	0.41	0.54	0.37	0.56	0.40	0.38	0.21	0.38	0.28
16	0.59	0.43	0.56	....	0.56	0.43	0.51	....	0.38	0.19	0.32	....
17	0 61	...	....	....	0.59	...	....	....	9.33	...	....	....
18	....	0.40	....	....	....	0.36	....	....	....	0.28	....	....

Arm Expanse.

The arm expanse was not found to differ to any great extent in the white children according to their different nationalities; it offers only individual variations. In the negroes the average arm expanse is greater at all ages.

In both the white and the negroes the arm expanse increases with the age of the children. Up to 9 years of age in the white boys and up to 11 years of age in the white girls the arm expanse is less than the total body height. In the negro children this is the case up to the seventh year of life. From 9 and 11 years on, in the white males and females, and from 7 years on, in the colored individuals, the arm expanse begins to surpass the body height, and the increase advances slightly with every year of life. This advance is more marked in the negroes.

A part of the increase of the arm expanse is not due to a greater growth of the arms themselves, but to the lateral growth of the thorax. This growth of the chest does not fully account for the differences in the arm-spread between the white and the negro children, and the arms of the colored individuals must be considered as really slightly longer than are those of the whites. I subjoin here a table which will illustrate the gradual increase of the proportion of the arm expanse to the total height in the different classes of children.

Per Cent. Relation of Average Arm Expanse to the Average Height, according to the ages of the Children.

AGE.	WHITE.		COLORED.	
	Male.	Female.	Male.	Female.
5	(96 7)	97.1	....	....
6	99.0	98.2	(98.8)	....
7	98.4	98.6	(99.6)	101.5
8	99.1	98.7	101.1	(98.6)
9	100.2	99.1	102.3	101.9
10	100.3	99.5	101.8	101.0
11	100.1	99.8	101.2	103.0
12	100.8	100.4	104.1	(98.7)
13	100.6	100 7	104.5	(105.5)
14	101.3	102.2	105.5	(102.1)
15	101.5	(100 0)	104.5	(103.4)
16	101.7	(102.1)	(107.1)	....
17	101.8	....	....	....

Measurements of the Chest.

After experimenting with various chest measurements it was found that the best satisfaction is obtained by restricting the measurements to diameters and taking these in all the children at the height of the nipples. The instrument with which the measurements were taken was a pair of accurate aluminum sliding compasses, with branches with broad surfaces. In measuring, the branches of the compass were applied not simply to touch the skin but until they met with a marked resistance on the body. Care was taken that the instrument should always be held diagonally to the long axis of the body. With care, measurements of this nature become quite accurate and satisfactory.

The results of the measuring, as will be seen from the appended figures, show first of all the growth of the chest during the different ages of the children.

In the second place, the figures demonstrate the differences which exist in the two proportions of the chest of the same height between the males and the females and between the white and the colored children.

Finally, calculations were made of the relation of the antero-posterior to the lateral diameter of the thorax at the different ages of the subjects measured, and these proportions or thoracic indexes, show the regular form of the chest, and the variations of this form, in the different ages of the children.

The size of the chest is greater on an average at all ages in the male than it is in the female children. This is the case in both the white and the colored subjects. When, however, we come to the females above 11 years of age, where the development of the breasts begins, the proportions of the chest will increase in the female and may surpass those of the male of the same age. This increase in depth of the female chest at or after puberty is due to additional deposition of fat and not to any changes in the osseous thorax.

In the colored children the chest is of very nearly the same size in the boys, but is somewhat smaller in the girls, than it is in corresponding sexes of white children. In both the colored boys and girls the chest is a little deeper than it is in the white children of corresponding sexes and ages. This difference lies in the thoracic cage itself.

The chest index shows at least one very interesting feature. In all classes of children the thorax is seen to be considerably deeper in early childhood than it is later. The increase of flatness takes place gradually and almost regularly through all the ages of the children, so far as our records go, with the exception of the females after the breast development takes place. The indices show very well the somewhat deeper character of the chest in the negro children, particularly the males. The flattening of the chest is most

4

rapid according to our figures between 3 and 7 years of age. This should probably read up to 7 years of age, as in the new-born infants the chest is almost equal in its anterio-posterior and its lateral diameter and it has already flattened considerably at the age of three, at which our figures begin.

Chest.

AGE.	WHITE.				COLORED.			
	DIAMETER ANTERO-POSTERIOR AT THE HEIGHT OF THE NIPPLES.		DIAMETER LATERAL AT THE HEIGHT OF THE NIPPLES.		DIAMETER ANTERO-POSTERIOR AT THE HEIGHT OF THE NIPPLES.		DIAMETER LATERAL AT THE HEIGHT OF THE NIPPLES.	
	Male.	Female.	Male.	Female.	Male.	Female.	Male.	Female.
5	12.55	11.95	17.10	17.25	....	....	....	....
6	13 74	13.31	18.73	18.22	13.20	....	17.40	....
7	14.27	13.14	19.63	18 56	13.10	12.65	18.10	18.00
8	14.28	13.39	19.87	19.05	14.94	14.30	19.56	17.40
9	14.56	13.93	20.59	19.92	14.83	14.18	20.10	20.64
10	14.83	14.26	21.07	20.82	15.07	13.40	21.00	19.70
11	15.24	14.59	21.64	21.24	15.24	14.18	21.23	20.45
12	15.68	14.35	22.31	21.83	15.41	17.15	21.90	24.15
13	16.13	15.74	23 07	23.03	15.77	16.20	22.43	24.40
14	16.78	17.07	23.70	23.79	17.46	15.95	24 07	22.80
15	16.94	17.38	24.42	25.10	16.32	17.45	22.95	25.20
16	18.53	16.40	27.16	25.50	17.20	....	24.55	....
17	18.83	....	26.13	....	....	....	....	....
18	....	15.70	....	23.40	....	....	....	....

Average Chest Index of the Children According to the Color, Sexes and Ages.

AGE.	WHITE.		COLORED.	
	Male.	Female.	Male.	Female.
5	(73.4)	(69.2)	....	....
6	73.4	73.0	(79.5)	....
7	71.9	70.2	(72.4)	(68.6)
8	72.0	70.3	72.3	....
9	70.8	70.0	74.1	68.7
10	70.0	69.4	71.6	(68.0)
11	70.5	68.7	72.8	69.2
12	70.3	65.4	70.6	(70.9)
13	70.0	68.4	69.6	....
14	70.8	71.6	72.5	(70.0)
15	69.3	(69.0)	71.3	(69.2)
16	68.4	....	(70.0)	....
17	(67.9)	....	....	....
18	....	....	....	....

The number of colored subjects represented in the above figures is small. If we include in this table, for the purpose of finding out with more certainty the relations of the chest index between the white and colored children, the data obtained on 100 additional colored children, obtained in the New York Colored Orphan Asylum, we obtain the following proportions:

Average Chest Index of the Children, According to the Color, Sexes and Ages, including the 100 Additional Children, from the N. Y. Colored Orphan Asylum.

AGE.	WHITE.		COLORED.	
	Male.	Female.	Male.	Female.
3	....	....	79.3	86.1
4	....	....	....	79.8
5	(73.4)	(69.2)	75.1	76.1
6	73.4	73.0	75.8	76.6
7	71.9	70.2	74.5	70.4
8	70.2	70.3	73.6	68.7
9	70.8	70.0	73.3	68.9
10	70.0	69.4	72.2	69.2
11	70.5	68.7	72.0	69.6
12	70.3	65.4	69.3	70.9
13	70.0	68.4	69.6	....
14	70.8	71.6	72.5	70.0
15	69.3	69.0	71.3	69.2
16	68.4	....	70.0	....
17	67.9	....	....	....

Measurements of the Head.

The principal diameters of the head differ largely according to the nationalities of the children and even in individuals. The main value of such dimensions of the head as the anterio-posterior or the lateral maximum diameters, and the height, lies in the correlation of same and in the resulting indices. The main value of the tables which show the individual measures, consists in the possibility of tracing the proportions of increase in these measures with the ages of the children, and then they show the differences in the averages between the males and the females, and between the white and the colored children.

The cephalic indices of the principal groups of the children in the asylum were already given at the end of the first part of these investigations. I add here the average indices calculated from age to age on all the children. These figures show the changes of the cephalic index with age. The relations of the length and of the width to the height of the head show nothing very extraordinary and as they would involve much additional technicalities, they will not be introduced here.

If we observe the averages of the different diameters in the following tables, we notice that the increase with age does not take place in all of them in the same way. The maximum anterioposterior diameter increases most, the maximum lateral diameter the least with the ages of the children. Thus, as children grow older their heads become relatively longer and their cephalic indices diminish. This fact is established by other observations on children, principally by Dr. Boas' investigations.

The measurements of the female head are throughout the smaller. Besides this, the differences in the lateral diameter of the head, between the two sexes of the children, are smaller in the female than are the differences in the two sexes in the anterio-posterior diameter. These facts show that the female head is totally smaller and, besides that, slightly more rounded than is the male head.

When we calculate the size of the head in proportion to the height of the body we still find that the female head is the smaller. The greater roundness of the female head is general in all races of people and at all ages.

The negro heads show, in the three principal diameters, a slight excess in size over the same measures in the white children; but we should remember that the colored children are found to be of an average greater height, which may account for the greater size of their head and of these diameters.

Average Diameter Antero-Posterior Max. of the Head of the Children, According to Color, Sexes and Ages.

AGE.	WHITE.		COLORED.	
	Male.	Female.	.	Female.
5	17.08	16.60	....	....
6	17.27	16.78	17.00	....
7	17.34	17.06	18.20	17.50
8	17.55	16.91	18.08	(16.00)
9	17.69	17 35	18.35	17.62
10	17.72	17.53	17.85	17.90
11	17.97	17.49	18 09	17.83
12	17.91	17.85	18.23	18 58
13	18.05	17.87	18.62	18.90
14	18.16	17.85	18.91	18.75
15	18.18	18.10	18.63	18.20
16	18.77	18.80	18.10	....
17	18.53	....	....	....
18	......	18.10	....	....

Average Diameter Lateral Maximum of the Head of the Children, According to Color, Sexes and Ages.

AGE.	WHITE.		COLORED.	
	Male.	Female.	Male.	Female.
5	13.75	14.00	....	....
6	13 94	13.56	13.60	........;
7	14.18	13.88	13.30	13.52
8	14.27	13.88	13 88	13 10
9	14.33	14.08	13 87	13.84
10	14.36	14.03	13.52	13.70
11	14.40	14.06	14.21	13.53
12	14.51	14.09	14.27	14.27
13	14.61	14.25	14.15	14.20
14	14.66	14.26	14.31	14.10
15	14.75	15.15	14.23	14.80
16	14.83	14.90	14 25	....
17	14.83	....	......	....
18	......	13.60	....	....

Average Height of the Head of the Children, According to Color, Sexes and Ages.

AGE.	WHITE.		COLORED.	
	Male.	Female.	Male.	Female.
5	12.40	11.60	....	....
6	12.71	12.09	12.50	........;
7	12.72	12 25	13.10	12.50
8	12.76	12 00	12.85	12.30
9	12.78	12.45	12.75	12.53
10	12.81	12.47	12.65	12.45
11	12.84	12.46	12.86	12.40
12	12.96	12.47	12.81	12.53
13	12.97	12.47	13.25	12.65
14	13.07	12.68	13.22	12.45
15	13.02	12 66	13.14	12.73
16	13.38	13.35	12.65	....
17	13.32	....	......	....
18	......	12.90	......	....

Average Cephalic Index of the Children According to Color, Sexes and Ages.

AGE.	WHITE.		COLORED.	
	Male.	Female.	Male.	Female.
5	80.5	84.3	......	....
6	80.7	80.8	80.0	....
7	81.7	81.3	73.1	77.2
8	81.2	82.1	76.7	81.9
9	81.0	81.1	75.6	78.5
10	81.0	80.0	76.8	76.5
11	80.1	80.4	78.5	75.8
12	81.0	78.9	78.3	76.8
13	80.9	79.7	76.0	75.1
14	80.7	79.8	75.8	75.2
15	81.1	83.7	76.3	81.3
16	79.0	79.2	78.7	....
17	80.0	......	......	....
18	......	75.1	......	....

The relative size and growth of the head can be illustrated in addition by the measure of the circumference of the head and by the so-called Smith's Module.

The circumference of the head is not a very favored measure in anthropology. The reasons for this are that it is often interfered with by the amount of hair of the individual measured, and that it has no relation to the height of the head, which may differ very widely. In children, where the height of the head does not differ as much as it does in adults, and where the hair forms but a very little obstacle to measuring, the circumference is a fairly valid measure. It shows by all means the gradual increase of the head with age of the children, and the differences in the size of the head among the different classes of children.

Average Head Circumference Maximum of the Children, According to Color, Sexes and Ages.

AGE.	WHITE.		COLORED.	
	Male.	Female.	Male.	Female.
5	50.20	49.35	......	....
6	51.67	49.13	50.50	....
7	51.38	50.20	51.80	50.80
8	51.61	49.80	52.32	47.00
9	51.97	50.78	52.60	52.34
10	52.03	51.31	51.15	52.55
11	52.50	51.12	52.49	50.13
12	52.58	51.92	53.06	54.40
13	53.00	51.93	53.77	53.70
14	53.37	52.81	54.27	53.10
15	53.30	54.30	54.10	54.40
16	54.82	54.80	52.75	....
17	53.93	....	......	....

The module of Smith is a term applied in anthropometry to an abstract number which is obtained by adding together the greatest length, the greatest width and the height of the head and dividing the resultant by 3. The figure obtained, although not expressing any real size of head, is nevertheless a very useful substitute for the real size or capacity of the cranium and is very useful in comparisons. Our table below, which gives the average modules of the different classes of children, shows how well we can trace the differences in the size of the head through these abstract figures. I prefer the module for this purpose to everything except the real cranial capacity, which, of course, can only be obtained on skulls.

Average Modules of the Head of the Children According to Color, Sexes and Ages.

AGE.	WHITE.		COLORED.	
	Male.	Female.	Male.	Female.
5	14.28	14.07	......	....
6	14.64	14.14	......	....
7	14.78	14.39	......	14.51
8	14.85	14.35	14.94	....
9	14.94	14.60	15.00	14.66
10	14.96	14.67	14.67	14.70
11	15.03	14.67	15.05	14.57
12	15.12	14.80	14.78	15.12
13	15.19	14.84	15.31	....
14	15.30	14.93	15 38	15.04
15	15.31	15.29	15.22	15.28
16	15.65	....	15 00	....
17	15.56	....	......	....
18	......	....	......	....

There are two more measurements of the head which deserve mention. The one is the Bin-Auricular diameter of the head, which shows the width of the head at about the height of the base of the brain and immediately in front of the ears, and the diameter frontal minimum, which shows the width of the base of the forehead. According to our figures, which are given below, the Bin-Auric Diameter differs much less in the two sexes of the children than is the case with any other measurement of the head that we have so far spoken of. In the colored children this diameter is always smaller than in the white children of corresponding ages; thus the skull of the negro child is absolutely narrower in this location, that is at the height of the base of the brain and immediately in front of the ear, than it is in white children.

Average Diameter Bin-Auric of the Children According to Color, Sexes and Ages.

AGE.	WHITE.		COLORED.	
	Male.	Female.	Male.	Female.
5	10.65	10.60	......	....
6	10.96	10.92	10.80	....
7	11.33	11.08	11.00	10.90
8	11.42	11.25	11.30	10.50
9	11.45	11.43	12.99	11.18
10	11.56	11.63	11.30	11.25
11	11.68	11.77	11.73	11.30
12	11.84	11.83	11.64	12.17
13	12.00	12.02	11.71	12.00
14	12.11	12.33	12.04	12.25
15	12.07	12.58	11.85	12.40
16	12.51	11.80	12.20	....
17	12.53	....	......	....
18	......	12.00	......	....

The diameter frontal minimum increases gradually with the ages in all of the children. The measure is generally smaller on the female heads. As to the differences in this measure between the white and the negroes our figures cannot be taken as conclusive as we have a too small a number of the colored children. Up to eleven years of age, according to our figures, the forehead of the negro child, both male and female, is on the average somewhat narrower than the forehead of the white child. After eleven years of age the conditions seem to be somewhat reversed. I am inclined to believe, if I consider all my observations on negroes together, that the average width of the forehead is generally slightly smaller in these than it is in the white people. In connection with the fact that the whole head of the negro is not smaller, this point would deserve a further investigation.

Average Diameter Front Minimum of the Children, According to Color, Sexes and Ages.

AGE.	WHITE.		COLORED.	
	Male.	Female.	Male.	Female.
5	9.10	9.45	......	....
6	9 73	9.35	9.50	....
7	9.78	9.53	9.40	9.37
8	9.84	9.59	9 90	9.00
9	10 07	9.70	9.85	9 78
10	9.97	9.86	9.72	9 90
11	10.14	9.83	10.11	9.73
12	10.05	10.13	10.26	10.33
13	10.20	10 06	10.78	10.30
14	10.29	10.27	10.55	10.25
15	10.24	10.45	10.33	10.70
16	10 62	10.30	10.10	....
17	10.23	....	......	....

The preceding figures conclude the study of the measurements of the children of the Juvenile Asylum. To review a few principal facts, these measures show that all the children of the institution taken as a class are apparently somewhat below the average of free, well nourished children in their growth.

The asylum children are of a somewhat smaller stature and smaller weight than are outside children that are available for comparison. It would be very interesting in this connection to know the differences between the children as they enter here and when they leave; perhaps it may be possible to learn this in future. Our measurements of the heads of the children show no great discrepancies from what we know is about the normal. There is good reason to believe that the majority of the inmates of the institution owe their slight physical inferiority only to malnutrition and neglect and not to inherent physical inferiority. These subjects cannot be excluded from the general average class of children. There is, however, a number of individuals here heavily charged with bad heredity, and their physical inferiority is to be referred to this inheritance; these individuals are exceptional.

Besides the above we have obtained some remarkable differences in the measurements of the white and the negro subjects. These data, even if they cannot be considered as decisive from these studies alone, are nevertheless valuable indications of the physical differences between the two classes of children.

PART III.

Physical Differences Between White and Colored Children of the Same Sexes and Ages.

The differences between the two classes of children may, in a resumé, be arranged into those which were observed equally in both sexes, and those which are prevalent in either the boys or the girls. Some of the characters in which the white and the black children differ were fairly well brought out in preceding parts of this study and will receive here but a passing notice. Other differences have not as yet been mentioned, and these will receive more consideration.

Differences Without Regard to the Sex or Age of the Children.

In a general way it can be stated that the white children present more diversity; the negro children more uniformity in all their normal physical characters. This becomes gradually more marked as the age of the children advances.

As to physical abnormalities, those of congenital origin are much less frequent in the negro child than they are in the white one; with acquired abnormalities, principally the results of rachitic conditions, the case is almost the reverse, those characters being less frequent in the white children.

In detail we find the following differences between the two classes of children:

Size of the Body.

The average height of the colored child is in all ages from one to three mm. greater than is the average height of white children, all the nationalities of these latter being taken together; it is still slightly greater when compared with the average height of only the American-born children, who are taller than the children of most other nationalities.

The average weight, unlike the height, is greater in the white children at all ages up to puberty; beyond puberty, particularly in the girls, the colored subjects seem to gain in weight more rapidly than do the white ones.

The size of the head is, on the average, slightly smaller in the negro children than it is in the white, provided we consider the size of the head in its relation to the size of the body. There are individual exceptions to this rule.

The form of the head is less variable in the colored children than it is in the American-born white children. A pure American colored child shows generally a pronounced dolichocephaly, whilst the normal white American child will show us everything from a marked long head to a pronounced brachycephaly. West Indies negro children are more frequently short-headed than those of North American origin.

The hair of the pure negro child is quite lusterless and as a rule either curly or wavy, by far more frequently the former than the latter. The proportion of wavy hair increases largely in mixed subjects and the same is true about luster of the hair. In white children, those of American origin especially, curly hair is found very seldom, and the curls always differ from those of the negro; they possess luster and will never show compact rouleaux arrangement. We do find curly hair among Jewish children and children born in southern European countries, and occasionally also among Teutonic people. Wavy hair is quite common among Jewish and Syrian subjects.

The forehead is on the average narrower at all ages in the negro child than it is in the white. The height of the forehead, however, is not smaller in the colored subject, and is occasionally even greater than it is in some of the white children.

The face of the colored children is generally more prognathic than is that of white children. The prognathism is both facial and alveolar.

The malar bones are somewhat more prominent in the colored child, but the difference is not so great as that which may be observed between a child of a yellow race and a white one.

The nose of the negro is frequently shorter and generally lower

FIG. 12.—A characteristic negro ear: small size, overhanging, compressed helix.

and broader than the nose of the white child. These differences increase somewhat with the age of the children.

The lips of the colored subjects are very prominent. This is partly due to the greater prognathism of the alveolar processes, but besides this the lips of the colored children are substantially thicker than are those of white children.

The mouth is broader and it is also more spacious antero-posteriorly in the negroes. This is due to the fact that in the colored child the palate is more spacious and longer than it is in the white.

The teeth of the negro children are often stronger than are those of white individuals. Irregularities in the setting of the teeth, which are so frequent in white children, are quite rare among the colored. Dentition in the colored is more regular.

The uvula is frequently shorter and stouter in the colored than it is in the white children, and is less frequently deflected in the former.

The lower jaw is often somewhat higher and the lower maxilla a little stronger in the colored subjects than it is in the white.

The ears of the colored deserve special notice. They show in many cases a marked and almost specific character, which is but rarely seen in the white. This character consists in that the helix is bent on itself and compressed at the highest fourth of the ear. The negro ear is also generally somewhat smaller in all its dimensions than the white one. In a certain proportion of cases the ears of the colored children are broader in the lower half than they are in the upper.

The body shows marked differences in the two classes of children, and some of these differences are more marked in children of certain ages than they are in adults. These differences are more marked in the female children than in the male.

In general the body of the negro child shows less adipose tissue and greater muscular development. The average strength in each arm, as measured by the dynamometer is greater, not only at all ages of the colored children, but also when calculated in proportion to every pound of weight of the body.

The pelvis of the colored child is more inclined forwards than that of the white child, and this is equally true in both sexes.

The arms of the colored child are longer than those of the white, and the arm-spread relatively to the height of the body is greater.

Both hands and feet, but especially the feet, are longer in the colored than they are in the white child. The feet are flatter in the colored. The thighs of the negro child show a remarkable difference from those of the white. They appear not unlike the thighs of a frog, being most prominent in the middle. This character is due largely to a higher forward and outward curvature of the thigh bone in the colored.

The calves are somewhat smaller in the negro child than they are in the white one.

Differences Peculiar to Boys.

The negro boy is generally well built, lean and muscular. The body, unlike that of many normal white boys, and unless deformed by disease, is plastic, straight and symmetrical. His chest is a little deeper.

The pelvis of the colored boy is more inclined and in consequence of this the lumbar curve is more pronounced, and the buttocks more prominent.

The penis of the colored boy is generally longer than that of a white boy of corresponding age or size.

Differences Peculiar to Female Children.

The colored girl, before the age of puberty, and sometimes even beyond this period, is a great deal more the shape of a boy than is the case with the white girl. Among white children, girls can be seen to show decided feminine characters; that is feminine shoulders and thorax, waist distinctly narrowed, large hips and fat thighs as early as 8 years of life. Among negro female children I have not seen these characters become manifest until after 12 years of age or even much later. When seen in profile the greater inclination of the pelvis in the female colored child becomes very apparent.

PART IV.

DIFFERENCES IN THE CHILDREN ACCORDING TO THEIR NATIONALITIES.

The differences in the children of different nationalities must be sought for principally in the measurements. All the differences must necessarily be considered separately at every age, and through this we are obliged to make so many separations of the children that several of the resulting groups of the boys and almost all the groups of the girls become insufficient for comparisons.

The positive results of the comparison of the measurements of the white children of the different nationalities will not be many, and none of those which we obtain can be looked on as definite, but are subject to further verification.

Had we sufficient numbers of children and no physically exceptional individuals among them, this part of the study would be anthropologically the most interesting one. As the matter stands, however, there are many defects to it.

The differences in the measurements of the children can be shown in the plainest way by a table in which the figures under the different headings represent the positions which the children of the different groups occupy in that particular respect in the total number of the age series. The figures will do more justice to children of most nationalities than they will do to Americans, a large proportion of whom come from families which are in various ways defective.

Average Positions Which the Children of Different Nationalities Occupy in the Total Number of the Age Series.

	Height.	Weight.	Pressure force.	Circumference of head.	Front diameter.	Height of head.
American	1	2	1	2	3	2
Irish	1	3	2	1	6	3
German	2	1	4	3	4	4
Italian	5	5	3	4	2	5
Russian	3	4	6	5	1	6
Syrian	4	6	5	6	5	1

I will not make many remarks about the above figures. The American children, notwithstanding the many physically inferior individuals among them, occupy the highest average position. Only next to them are the Irish, and the Germans follow very closely. The Russian Jews and the Syrians are physically the most inferior of the children.

Among the few single remarkable facts are (a) the unevenness of the relations of the weight and force of the children of the different nationalities; (b) the disproportion between the circumference of the head and the width of the forehead in Irish children; (c) a disproportion in the same figures, but of opposite nature with the Russian Jews; (d) the highest weight with a second-class height and fourth-class force in the Germans; (e) the height of the head in the Syrians.

According to the preceding figures the American and the Irish children are the tallest; the Germans are the heaviest; the Americans are the most powerful; the Irish children have the largest circumference of the head, but at the same time the smallest width of the forehead, while the forehead is widest in the Russian Jews and the Italians; in the height of the head the first place belongs to the Syrians.

PART V.

Separate Report on the Entirely Normal Children.

There were found, as stated already before, among the 1,000 children examined in the asylum, 58 white boys, 35 white girls, 5 colored boys and 7 colored girls, on whose bodies there was not found even a single pronounced abnormality.

Of the white children, 8 boys and 1 girl were born of American parents, 20 boys and 24 girls born of Italian parents, 10 boys and 2 girls were of German, and 8 boys and 1 girl of Russian origin. The remaining children out of the 58 boys and 35 girls were divided in small numbers among various nationalities.

If we reduce the above numbers to percentages, we obtain for the American boys 13.8 per cent.; for the girls 2.85 per cent. of physically normal children from the whole number of children of this nationality examined. For the Italian boys, similar proportions are 34.5 per cent.; for the Italian girls 68.6 per cent.; for the German boys 17.2 per cent.; for the girls 5.7 per cent.; and for the Russian boys 13.8 per cent.; for the girls 2.85 per cent. of the total. Now, among the total of white children, these four nationalties were represented as follows:

	Boys. %	Girls. %
American	21.1	9.8
Italian	33.2	61.2
German	14.6	9.1
Russian	8.8	2.1

If we compare the two classes of percentages we see that the entirely normal American children are proportionately much less frequent to the whole percentage in the institution than are any of the other three groups of children. The reason for this, in my opinion, lies in the fact that many of the children of foreigners are sent to the institution for poverty simply and may proceed from parents who are physically and otherwise entirely normal. Children of American parents, on the other hand, are more frequently sent here for real destitution, or as a result of various transgressions and such children are more liable to proceed from parents who are themselves not physically normal and who left to their children as an inheritance various physical irregularities and predispositions.

The family history of the children who are without any physical abnormalities is very clear. Among the parents of all these 105 children only 2 persons were intemperate, 2 persons insane, and 2 persons who deserted the family. In 60 instances among the white children, and in 2 instances among the colored, both of the parents of the child were still living, and in only 4 cases of the white and 3 cases of the colored children were both parents dead. Among the causes of death of the deceased parents, so far as we could ascertain, 9 persons died of consumption, 2 of meningitis, and all the remaining of acute diseases or of accidents.

The measurements of the children without any physical abnormalities, when compared with the average measurements of all the children who are in the institution, are almost generally, at least so with the boys, superior. This point will be best appreciated by the perusal of the following table:

Boys—White.

(1) All.   (2) Physically entirely normal.

AGE.	HEIGHT.		WEIGHT.		PRESSURE FORCE, RIGHT HAND.		PRESSURE FORCE, LEFT HAND.		CIRCUMFERENCE OF HEAD.		DIAMETER FRONTAL MINIMUM.	
	1	2	1	2	1	2	1	2	1	2	1	2
	mm.	mm.	lbs.	lbs.	lbs.	lbs.	lbs.	lbs.	cm.	cm.	cm.	m.
5	961	971	33	32.0	10	12	10	10	50.20	49.6	9.10	8.90
8 ...	1152	1052	47	39.7	20	16	18	16	51.60	51.0	9.84	9.30
9	1212	1232	53	56.0	24	28	24	28	51.97	52.55	10.07	10.20
10	1248	1258	57	58.4	28	28.5	26	27	52.00	52.6	9.97	10.12
11	1315	1360	64	73.0	32	38	30	36	52.50	53.2	10.14	10.40
12	1362	1343	70	65.2	36	34.5	34	33	52.58	52.0	10.05	9.93
13	1420	1482	81	89.8	40	47.5	38	44	53.00	53.55	10 20	10.50
14	1449	1464	84	91.5	44	49	40	46	53.37	54 4	10.29	10.50
15	1462	1497	85	97.0	48	56	46	50	53.30	54.1	10.24	10.20

Girls—White.

(1) All. (2) The physically entirely normal.

AGE.	Height.		Weight.		Pressure Force, Right Hand.		Pressure Force, Left Hand.		Circumference of Head.		Diameter Frontal Minimum.	
	1	2	1	2	1	2	1	2	1	2	1	2
	mm.	mm.	lbs.	lbs.	lbs.	lbs.	lbs.	lbs.	cm.	cm.	cm.	cm.
7	1088	1134	42	43	12	12	12	11.5	50.2	50.7	9.53	9.8
8	1130	1057	45	36 6	16	13	16	10.5	49.8	48.9	9.59	9.5
9	1187	1170	52	50.5	18	18	16	16	50.78	50.7	9.7	9.8
10	1267	1264	60	58	24	22.5	22	21	51.3	51.3	9.86	9.9
11	1304	1312	65	66	26	28.5	24	25.5	51.1	51.6	9.83	9.8
13	1431	1417	84	81.5	36	32	32	31	51.9	51.7	10.1	10.1

Teeth.

In addition to the examination of the body, limbs and other previously mentioned parts, attention was given also to the condition of the teeth of the children. Among this class of individuals the condition of the teeth was found to be *fine*,* that is there were no more decayed and absent teeth in the mouth than up to two, in 54, or 53 per cent. of the cases. The teeth were *good*, that is, there were between two and six lost and decayed, in 36 per cent. of the cases. The teeth were *mediocre*, that is, there were lost and decayed more than six but less than a half of the total number, in a little over 9 per cent. of the cases; and of *bad* teeth, or those where a half or more of the total number were lost and decayed, there were three cases, or about 3 per cent. of the total.

Careful inquiries were made with the teachers and attendants of the children as to their abilities in learning and as to their characters since they have been under observation. From the data thus collected it appears that there were among these children 87, or 83 per cent., with abilities that could be said to be about the average for children of the same ages outside the institution. In 3 per cent. of the cases the abilities of the children were decidedly superior; and in 14 per cent. the abilities were in some way inferior to the general average. Almost half of the children with inferior abilities in learning had some known bad heredity.

* The denominations used here are entirely arbitrary, but I have used them extensively in examining different classes of people and find them very satisfactory.

As to the character of this class of children, this can be judged of in two ways; first, by the cause of commitment to the institution, and, second, by the conduct of the child since confinement. This second criterion is undoubtedly the safer.

As to the cause of coming here, as stated on admission of the children, we find that 13 individuals of the whole number of 105 were sent here for truancy, 9 for disobedience, 2 for running away, 1 for staying out late, 1 for begging, 1 for petty larceny, 1 for pilfering, and 3 for being ungovernable. All these together amount to 30 per cent. of the 105 children, the remaining 70 per cent. came here either for a home or on account of poverty of their parents or guardians.

Observation of the children since they have been in the institution shows that 3, only, out of the 105, behaved persistently badly. Two of these individuals had at the same time inferior learning abilities and bad heredity.

The conclusion which can be made from the above data is, that the physically entirely normal children are liable both to be children with little heredity predisposition, and with fairly normal abilities and character. These facts will be much better appreciated after several of the following sections of this study have been perused by the reader. That there should be found among the children who have no physical abnormalities a certain percentage with inferior abilities and with a persistent bad behavior, shows that the mental system can not be looked at as a mere reflection of the state of the body, or the reverse; the brain can apparently have properties which are not perceptible in the external parts of the individual.

PART VI.

CHILDREN WITH FIVE OR MORE ABNORMALITIES.

There were found of such children 62 white males, 16 white females, 8 colored males and 1 colored female, in all 87.

The measures of these children show that almost 50 per cent. of the individuals of this class (48.3 per cent.) are in their principal measurements below the general average obtained on all the children of similar ages in the institution. The following table shows a comparison of the principal average measurements of the abnormal white boys with those obtained on all the white boys in the institution.

Boys—White.

(1) All (2) Boys with 5 or more abnormalities.

AGE.	HEIGHT.		WEIGHT.		PRESSURE FORCE. RIGHT HAND.		PRESSURE FORCE. LEFT HAND.		CIRCUMFERENCE OF HEAD.		DIAMETER FRONT MINIMUM.	
	1	2	1	2	1	2	1	2	1	2	1	2
	mm	mm	lbs.	lbs.	lbs.	lbs	lbs.	lbs.	cm.	cm.	cm.	cm.
6	1051	1120	40	45	14	16	12	14	51.67	52.0	9.73	9.9
7	1120	1113	45	45	18	20	16	18	51.38	51.4	9.78	9.7
8	1152	1181	47	48	20	20	18	18	51.61	51.4	9.84	9.9
9	1212	1205	53	52	24	26	24	24	51.97	50.9	10.07	9.8
10 ...	1248	1247	57	51	28	22	26	22	52.03	51.5	9.97	9.7
11 ...	1315	1306	61	62	32	32	30	30	52.50	53.2	10.14	9.9
12 ...	1362	1369	70	70	36	34	34	32	52.58	53.2	10.05	10.1
13 ...	1420	1420	81	76	40	42	38	38	53.00	52.5	10.20	9.8
14 ...	1449	1478	81	84	44	44	40	42	53.37	53.2	10.29	10.2
15 ...	1462	1422	85	74	48	42	46	38	53.30	53.6	10.24	10.1
16 ...	1615	1606	115	107	68	66	53	64	51.82	54.5	10.62	10.5

Inquiries as to the nationalities of these children show that 21 or about 27 per cent. of the white boys were of American parentage, 24 or about 31 per cent. were Italians, and 11 or about 14 per cent. were Germans. The proportion of abnormal children is much smaller among the Italians than is the proportion of the children of this nationality to the total of white children in the institution. Of the Germans it is about the same, but of the Americans it is considerably greater. These facts are to be explained on the same basis as I mentioned in connection with the children who were entirely free from physical abnormalities.

There were made similar inquiries as to the ability at learning and character of the children who show many abnormalities, as were made with the other groups of children. Pains were taken to secure these data as reliable as possible.

These inquiries reveal that, as to ability at learning, there are only 55 or about 63 per cent. of the children of this class who are in this respect up to the average of public school children, 28 individuals, or a little over 32 per cent., are of inferior abilities, while four children are exceptionablly bright. It would seem from these figures that numerous abnormalities of the body stand frequently in connection with inferior abilities of the mind. However, such a combination is far from general, and occasionally a body offering many abnormalities is associated with very good mental powers.

As to the character of the children of this class, so far as we can judge from the causes which brought the child here, it is inferior to the children who are physically free of abnormalities. The percentage of children with five or more abnormalities who were sent to the asylum for some bad conduct was 30 per cent. of the total, which is an equal proportion to that which we have seen with the physically normal children. But there are two points of difference between the two classes of individuals. In the first place, almost all the younger children with many abnormalities, that is children below 10 years of age, were sent here for destitution. Out of the remaining children of this class, that is, those after 10 years of age, a very great proportion were misbehaved individuals. This fact was noticed to a much smaller extent among children free from physical defects. The second point of difference consists in the character of the offences. I gave in Part V the offences of the physically normal individuals. They were: in 12.4 per cent. of the 105 normal children truancy; in 8.6 per cent. disobedience; in 3 per cent. ungovernable; in 2 per cent. running away; in 1 per cent. each staying out, begging, petit larceny and pilfering. Of the 87 children with five or more abnormalities: in 11.5 per cent. of the cases the children were brought here for disobedience; in 10.3 per cent. for truancy; in 5.7 per cent. for petit larceny; in 1.15 per cent. for pilfering and in 1.15 per cent. burglary. The character of the offences on the whole was more grave with the physically defective children.

As to the behavior of the children of this class since under observation in the asylum, their conduct was stated to be persistently bad in some way in 15 cases, or 17 per cent. of the total.

It seems, whatever causes there may be for the fact, that the children with numerous physical abnormalities are also more liable to abnormalities of character than are the children who are physically entirely normal. The phenomenon may perhaps be explained from two main standpoints. On the one hand, the child with numerous abnormalities carries in the majority of the cases more serious predisposition inherited from its parents, and this predisposition affects not only its body but also diminishes its energy and self control. Besides this, children whose parents were physically inferior have undoubtedly suffered more from neglect and from insufficient training, as a class, than children whose parents we have reason to believe were physically normal, and these conditions have left a mark on their character.

In illustration of this last point we find that among the 87 children, in seven cases both of the parents were dead, in 22 cases the father alone and in 13 cases the mother alone were dead.

The kind of heredity these children have received is shown well enough by the number of their dead parents, but it illustrated in addition, even from the scarce information we have in this respect, by the fact that 12 of the parents of the children were intemperate, 3 deserted their family, and 1 was a forger.

The children who show many physical abnormalities should not be condemned and looked upon as any inferior beings, simply because of their physical abnormalities. But it should be borne in mind that many of these children may require an additional and prolonged care. With such care the majority of them will develop into good members of the community.

PART VII.

CHILDREN WHO WERE CRIMINAL OR VICIOUS.

In this class we find 72 males and only 5 females. The preponderance of the males over the females among the children with decidedly bad characters is remarkable.

The measure table of the criminal or vicious children given below will show that there is no general physical inferiority to be observed in these children as a class. To this there are, however, individual exceptions.

White—Males.

(1) All.   (2) Children who are criminal or vicious.

AGE.	HEIGHT.		WEIGHT.		PRESSURE FORCE, RIGHT HAND.		PRESSURE FORCE, LEFT HAND.		CIRCUMFERENCE OF HEAD.		DIAMETER, FRONTAL MINIMUM.	
	1	2	1	2	1	2	1	2	1	2	1	2
	mm.	mm.	lbs.	lbs	lbs.	lbs.	lbs.	lbs.	cm.	cm.	cm.	cm.
10....	1248	1234	57	56	28	28	26	27.2	52.03	51.5	9 97	9.9
11....	1315	1339	64	67.9	32	34.2	30	32.2	52.50	53.0	10.14	10.1
12 ...	1362	1375	70	72	36	40	34	36	52.58	53.1	10.05	10.1
13....	1420	1417	81	77	40	42	38	38	53.00	52.8	10.20	10.0
14....	1449	1467	84	85	44	44	40	40.4	53 37	53.2	10.29	10.1
15....	1462	1482	85	91	48	50.6	46	48	53.30	53.8	10.24	10.4
16....	1615	1610	115	114	68	66	53	62	54.82	54.9	10.62	10.4
17....	1654	1720	122	133	74	89	72	84	53.93	54.6	10.23	10.6

As to the parentage of this class of children in 19 cases, or 27.5 per cent., the white individuals were of American parentage. (This fact accounts to a certain extent for the value of some of the average physical measurements.) In 18 instances, or 26 per cent., the children were of German parentage, and in 14 instances, or 20 per cent., these children were Russian Jews. There was no Syrian among these individuals and, what is very remarkable, considering the number of children of this nationality in the institution, there was only *one* Italian. The preponderance of American children among the criminal and vicious children must be referred to the same causes which I mentioned in connection with the entirely normal children.

There was found a lesser proportion of abnormalities to each of
the children of this class than we will find to be the case with children
of some of the following groups. Nevertheless, the proportion is
slightly above the general averages in the institution. There were
to each white boy 3.1 of abnormalities; to each white girl 2.5; to each
colored male 2.6, while the 1 colored female was entirely normal.
Among the total of 231 abnormalities of all classes there were 41, or
about 17 per cent. of serious nature, and 70, or a little over 30 per
cent., of indifferent nature, while the remaining 120 were of medium
significance. Additionally, in three cases there was observed a
serious condition of the heart.

If we consider the above data on the criminal and vicious children
in the institution, and then compare them with similar data obtained from other groups of children here reported, we must come
to the conclusion that the misbehaved children are not characterized
as a class by any considerable physical inferiority, or by any great
proportion of physical abnormalities; nor have I found that any
particular atypical character could be said to be characteristic of
this class of individuals. In consequence it seems to me the causes
for the bad conduct and character of many of the children of this
class must be attributed, so far as we can see, not so much to their
constitution as to the social circumstances and environment to which
they were subjected.

As to the teeth, they were found in 31 per cent. of the criminal
or vicious children to be in fine condition; in 51 per cent. of the
cases they were good; in 14.3 per cent. of the cases they were
mediocre, and in 2.6 per cent. they were bad. The condition of the
teeth is inferior in these subjects to the conditions found in the
physically entirely normal children.

The itemized causes of the commitment of the individuals of this
class are as follows: Admitted as ungovernable, 25; for petit larceny, 24; for pilfering, 12; for burglary, 6; for stealing, 3; for
assault, 2; for attempted theft, 2; for grand larceny, 1; for pocket
picking, 1; and for an attempt at burglary, 1.

Since these children have been in the asylum, 75, out of a total
of 77, were found to be entirely tractable and have behaved in a
satisfactory way. The remaining 2 show, both, sneaking disposition, cowardice and a tendency to lying.

As to the abilities at learning of the criminal or vicious children, 10 out of 77, or 13 per cent., were found with inferior abilities; in 2 cases the children were extraordinarily bright; and in 65 cases, or 85 per cent. of the total, the abilities were equal to the average ability of children outside the institution.

I may mention in this connection that I have considerable confidence in the data as to the ability of the children, for many of the teachers in the institution have had a long experience in teaching in the public schools.

It may be interesting to remark that out of the 10 children with inferior abilities of learning, 6 were committed for larger transgressions (3 pilfering, 1 assault, 1 petit larceny, 1 burglary); the remaining 4 were ungovernable.

Taking all the above data on this class of children into consideration, I think that the criminal and vicious subjects show very favorably, and with the proper treatment give great hopes as to their future. What seems to me of the greatest importance in connection with these children is that their sojourn in the asylum should be sufficiently prolonged so that the good new habits may become a part of the nature of these children. With such treatment I think this class would turn out exceedingly few inveterate criminals.

PART VIII.

CHILDREN WHOSE PARENTS WERE INTEMPERATE, CRIMINAL, INSANE OR DISSOLUTE.

This class of children carries undoubtedly not only many defects, the result of bad inheritance, but also the consequences of bad environment. We find altogether 61 of such children in the institution; 24 of these are native born, 9 are colored children born in this country, and 28 are partly or wholly foreign.

Members of this class of children come into the Asylum, almost as a rule, very young and generally for destitution, being early abandoned, or left orphans by their parents.

In measurements children of this class are generally inferior to children with normal inheritance. Almost 60 per cent. of the individuals of this class were found to be inferior in their principal measurements to the general averages of the corresponding classes of the asylum children. The following comparative table shows these differences better than words could.

Boys—White.

(1) All.   (2) Those whose parents were insane, intemperate, dissolute or criminal.

AGE.	HEIGHT.		WEIGHT.		PRESSURE FORCE, RIGHT HAND.		PRESSURE FORCE, LEFT HAND.		CIRCUMFERENCE OF HEAD.		DIAMETER FRONT MINIMUM.	
	1	2	1	2	1	2	1	2	1	2	1	2
	mm.	mm.	lbs.	lbs.	lbs.	lbs.	lbs.	lbs.	cm.	cm.	cm.	cm.
5	961	951	33	34	10	10	10	8	50.2	50.8	9.10	9.3
6	1051	1023	40	36	14	11.5	12	10.5	51.67	51.2	9.73	9.9
7	1120	1071	45	39	18	12.5	16	10	51.38	50.6	9.78	9.8
8	1152	1187	47	47	20	20	18	18	51.61	50.9	9.84	9.6
9	1212	1217	53	50	24	24	24	22	51.97	51.8	10.07	9.9
10	1248	1233	57	51.6	28	27	26	25	52.03	51.8	9.97	9.9
11	1315	1244	64	58.0	32	29	30	27.6	52.50	51.4	10.14	9.6
12	1362	1348	70	64.7	36	34	34	31	52.58	51.6	10 05	9.65
13	1420	a 1388 b 1642	81	a 75 b 124	40	a 40 b 50	38	a 36 b 50	53.00	a 52.0 b 55.4	10.20	a 10.0 b 10.9
14	1449	1401	81	71	44	36	40	32	53.37	52.1	10.29	10.6
15	1462	1444	85	81	48	47.5	46	43.5	53.30	53.7	10.24	10.3
17	1654	1506	122	100	74	46	72	46	53.93	53.7	10.23	9.5

a and b represent two individuals.

The children whose parents were intemperate, insane, etc., are burdened with numerous physical abnormalities. The proportions of abnormalities to each child of this class were as follows: In white boys, 3.33; in white girls, 2.44; in colored boys, 3.75 and in colored girls, 2.20 to each individual. These proportions are above those which were obtained on all the children of the same sexes and color in the asylum together. Out of a total of 185 abnormalities 45 or about 24 per cent. were of a serious character, while 31 per cent. were of more or less indifferent nature. There were among these 61 children observed in addition, 5 cases of disturbances of the heart, of which at least one was serious.

The teeth in this class of subjects are in a condition much inferior to that found in the physically normal children. Fine teeth were found in only 23 per cent. of the cases, good teeth in 54 per cent. mediocre teeth in 20 per cent. and bad teeth in 3.2 per cent. of the 61 cases.

Among the causes of admission of this class of children, we find that 56 out of the 61 individuals were brought here for destitution. Of the others, 3 were sent here for disobedience, 1 for pilfering and 1 for truancy. As most of the individuals of this class have to be sent here very early for destitution, there has been but very little time for them to develop or show fully an abnormal character.

While inside of the institution 52 of the children behaved well, 9 or about 15 per cent. of the class showed a persistent bad character. This proportion of persistently badly behaved individuals under confinement is not equalled in any other class of children in the asylum.

As to the abilities at learning of this class of subjects, this shows also worse than in any other class of children in the institution. In almost 28 per cent. of the cases the ability of these children is distinctly inferior. In 3 individuals there were observed special brightness or ability in some directions, while abilities approaching the average of outside children exists only in 41 or in about 67 per cent. of the total.

Thus the children who carry a serious burden of heredity are found as a class and with very few exceptions as individuals to be in

many particulars inferior, not only to entirely normal children but
even to the average child of the institution and even to the simple
orphans.   Of all the classes of children the treatment of this one
appears to me to be the least hopeful.   No individuals of this sort
should be discharged from the asylum except after a prolonged stay
and only when they can be placed in much superior conditions than
were those from which they came.

PART IX.

ORPHANS OR CHILDREN WHOSE BOTH PARENTS ARE DEAD.

Of this class of individuals there were found 38 in all in the asylum. In all probability many of these individuals carry some serious hereditary predisposition. About 40 per cent. of these children were found to be subaverage in their principal physical measurements. I will give here a few rows of figures which will show the differences in the measurements of this class of children from the general averages obtained on all the white children of the same sex in the asylum. Only the boys are in a sufficient number to be compared.

Boys—White.

(1) All. (2) Children whose both parents are dead.

AGE.	HEIGHT.		WEIGHT.		PRESSURE FORCE. RIGHT HAND.		PRESSURE FORCE. LEFT HAND.		CIRCUMFERENCE OF HEAD.		DIAMETER FRONTAL MINIMUM.	
	1	2	1	2	1	2	1	2	1	2	1	2
	mm.	mm.	lbs.	lbs.	lbs.	lbs.	lbs.	lbs.	cm.	cm.	cm.	cm.
8....	1152	1136	47	43.5	20	18	18	15	51.6	52.6	9.84	10.2
10....	1248	1232	57	53.5	28	26	26	24	52.0	53.0	9.97	10.4
11....	1315	1320	64	66	32	32.5	30	31.5	52.5	53.5	10.14	10.1
12....	1362	1324	70	64.6	36	32	34	31	52.58	52.2	10.05	10.1
13....	1420	1413	81	77	40	38	38	36	53.0	52.8	10.20	10.2
14....	1449	1481	84	87	44	50	40	38	53.37	53.9	10.29	10.2

In the number of their abnormalities the orphan children exceed the general averages found in the asylum. Thus among the boys of this class the proportion of abnormalities to each child was 3.2; in the white female, 2.2; in the colored male, 4.25; in the colored female, 2.5. Most of these proportions are somewhat above those which we have seen in Part I, and which were obtained on the total numbers of the children of same sexes and color. Out of the total of 121 abnormalities of all kinds found on the 38 orphan children, 28 or about 23 per cent. were of serious character, while 30 or about 25 per cent. were indifferent abnormalities.

The teeth in the orphan children were found in 40 per cent. of the cases to be fine, in 45 per cent. to be good and in 16 per cent. of cases to be mediocre. If we compare these figures with similar figures obtained on the physically entirely normal children, we will find that the teeth of the orphans in the institution are not up to the standard of these latter.

Character of the Children.—Almost all the younger children of this class are sent here on account of poverty. Among the older individuals the lack of parental care, and probably also some of the hereditary predisposition the children carry, shows itself in a large percentage of misconduct. Out of a total of 38 children, 14, or about 37 per cent., were committed here for either disobedience, (9); running away, (2); petit larceny, (2), or stealing, (1). As all these misbehaved children were males, the real proportion rises to 45 per cent. If we should only consider individuals above 10 years of age, the proportion of misbehaved would be very great.

As to their abilities at learning, the orphan children do not show anything extraordinary. Three or about 8 per cent. of them were of inferior abilities in learning, 1 was of a superior ability and 34 were about the average of outside children.

Three only of the children of this class were persistently either destructive, dishonest, or vicious, since they have been confined in the institution. The character of the others shows nothing perverse, which is a sign that the badness of the children of this class before they came into the asylum was more due to acquisition by habits than to any inherent moral defects. Apparently the sooner the children of this class are sent to the institution, the better.

PART X.

CHILDREN WHOSE ONE OR BOTH PARENTS DIED OF CONSUMPTION.

There were found 51 of these children in the institution. Forty per cent. of these were inferior in their physical measures. The accompanying table shows the principal measures of the boys of consumptive parents compared with the general averages obtained on all the white boys in the institution.

Boys—White.

(1) All. (2) Children both of whose parents died of consumption.

AGE.	HEIGHT.		WEIGHT.		PRESSURE FORCE, RIGHT HAND.		PRESSURE FORCE, LEFT HAND.		CIRCUMFERENCE OF HEAD.		DIAMETER FRONT MINIMUM.	
	1	2	1	2	1	2	1	2	1	2	1	2
	mm.	mm.	lbs	lbs.	lbs.	lbs.	lbs.	lbs.	cm.	cm.	cm.	cm.
8	1152	1116	47	42.5	20	16	18	13	51.61	51.1	9.84	9.8
9	1212	1218	53	55	24	26	24	24.4	51.97	51.9	10.07	9.9
10	1248	1244	57	53	28	23.5	26	21	52.03	51.1	9.97	9.9
11	1315	1275	64	61.6	32	34	30	32	52.50	53.5	10.14	10.2
12	1362	1324	70	63.4	36	31.2	34	30	52.58	51.3	10.05	9.8
13	1420	1397	81	77	40	39.6	36	38	53.00	53.3	10.20	10.4
14	1449	1439	84	80	44	41.2	40	36.4	53.37	52.7	10.29	9.9

The proportion of abnormalities to each child in this class is greater than the proportion found on all the children together. Thus there were to each white boy of this class 2.83 of abnormalities; to each white girl 3.3; to each colored boy 5.3; to each colored girl 2. (Compare with similar figures on all the children in Part I.) Of the total of 155 abnormalities of all kinds found in the children of consumptive parents, 39, or 25 per cent., were of a serious character, and but 41, or 26 per cent., were of indifferent nature. Besides this, in 5 cases, there were found defects of the heart.

The condition of the teeth in all this class of children was found to be as follows: In 23 per cent. of the cases the teeth were fine; in 61 per cent. they were good; in 16 per cent. of the instances the teeth were mediocre. The condition of the teeth in the children of consumptive parents is considerably inferior to the condition of the teeth in the children who are physically entirely normal.

The character of the children of consumptive parents is not very encouraging. Twenty-three, or 45 per cent., of these children were brought to the institution for some sort of misconduct. In 14 instances the misconduct was disobedience, in 7 cases truancy, in 1 staying out, and in 1 petit larceny. In 2 of the children the behavior since they have been in the asylum is bad. In 1 boy the speech is very defective.

Thirteen and seven-tenths per cent. of the children whose one or both parents died of consumption were of inferior abilities in learning, and no one of the 51 children showed in any way an exceptional brightness.

Both the ordinary orphans and the orphans whose parents we know succumbed to consumption are shown in these last two divisions to be physically inferior, not only to entirely normal children, but also to the average of all the asylum children taken together. In both classes, besides, there is apparent a considerable tendency for misconduct. The physical inferiority of these individuals is undoubtedly due to a very large extent to the inherited deficiencies in their constitution. The tendency to misbehavior may be partly due to some deficiencies, but is in all probability much more due to improper training and other causes of social character, which were the results of the decease of the parents of the children. The similarity in the data concerning both of these classes of orphans is undoubtedly due to the fact that in each of the classes there are many individuals who at the same time belong also to the other division.

CONCLUSION.

It seems to me that the most proper way to conclude this study will be not by any generalizations, but with a wish for the extension of similar investigations. There is a broad and promising field for studies of this nature in Juvenile Asylums, as well as in other institutions in this country, and particularly in the State of New York. If I were allowed a suggestion, I would recommend that the State Boards of Charities, particularly that of this State, give their official sanction and support to such studies, and extend them gradually to correctional and other institutions which fall under their control; *provided, of course, that they can secure the services of the proper, able and unprejudiced, investigators.*

INDEX.

www.ingramcontent.com/pod-product-compliance
Lightning Source LLC
Chambersburg PA
CBHW030543270326
41927CB00008B/1495